THE LOVE TRIANGLE:
SEX, DATING, & LOVE

RONALD L. KOTESKEY

VICTOR BOOKS ®
A DIVISION OF SCRIPTURE PRESS PUBLICATIONS INC.
USA CANADA ENGLAND

THE LOVE TRIANGLE: SEX, DATING, & LOVE takes a frank, informative, biblically based look at the troubling issues of sexuality, relationships, and love as they affect teenagers today. Student activity booklets (Rip-Off Sheets) and a leader's guide with visual aids (SonPower Multiuse Transparency Masters) are available from your local Christian bookstore or from the publisher.

Scripture taken from the *Holy Bible, New International Version,* © 1973, 1978, 1984, International Bible Society. Used by permission of Zondervan Bible Publishers. Other Scripture quotations are from the *King James Version* (KJV).

Library of Congress Catalog Card Number: 89-60137

ISBN: 0-89693-755-0

Recommended Dewey Decimal Classification: 248.83
Suggested Subject Heading: YOUTH—RELIGIOUS LIFE

CONTENTS

1

THE TRIANGLE

Three teenage couples went to see the same movie on the same day. The first couple was Celeste and Frazer. (They weren't officially a "couple," since this was only their second date, but the two of them went to the movie together.)

They had a good time at the movie, got a bite to eat afterward, and returned to Celeste's house about 11 P.M. After parking the car, Frazer turned to Celeste and said, "I love you."

Celeste didn't know what to say, but she'd enjoyed their two dates so she mumbled something like, "I like you too, Frazer."

As Frazer gave her a good-night kiss in the car, Celeste felt his hands getting too friendly with her body. Feeling uncomfortable, she quickly said good-night, got out of the car, and hurried into her house.

The second couple who went to see the movie was Greta and Forrest. They had been going together for nearly seven months. After the movie they went to Forrest's house.

There was no hesitation in saying "I love you" by either Greta or Forrest as they got into bed together.

When they were done making love, Forrest rolled over and looked at his alarm clock. "We've got to get out of here!" he exclaimed. "Mom will be home in half an hour! If she catches us, she'll go through the roof!"

They hurriedly got dressed. Fifteen minutes later, Greta was home.

The third couple who went to see the movie was Linda and Rod. They got married the week after high school graduation, and now had a three-month-old daughter. This was their first night out since the baby had been born.

Like Celeste and Frazer, they arrived home about 11 P.M. After Rod took the baby-sitter home, he and Linda showered and climbed into bed together. Rod turned to Linda, smiled at her, and said, "I love you. I'm so glad you married me."

Linda didn't hesitate to tell Rod that she loved him and was happy to be married to him too. Lying in bed together, they talked about what the baby would be like when she grew up. They talked about how they would change her room around soon when they got her a bed instead of the crib. Then, in the closeness of the moment, they made love and fell asleep together.

What similarities and differences were there in the experiences of these three imaginary couples? In each case, the couple went on a "date"; in each case, something was mentioned about "love"; and in each case, the couple had to deal with the issue of "sex." However, the issues of "sex," "dating," and "love" were handled in different ways by the three couples.

Before getting into the specifics of sex, dating, and love, let's examine what role these three issues play in your life.

SELF-EXAMINATION

To make this discussion more personal, fill out the following "Sex, Dating, & Love Scale." Psychologists have developed several methods for measuring love and romance, and the following scale is built on some of these methods. Fill in the blanks with the name of the special person in your life. If you aren't married or seriously dating someone, fill in the name of someone you like. (You may want to write on a separate piece of paper so that others reading the book won't see your answers.)

SEX, DATING, & LOVE SCALE

Circle the number that indicates your response to each of the following questions.

> 0 = Strongly disagree/never
> 1 = Disagree/seldom
> 2 = Unsure/sometimes
> 3 = Agree/often
> 4 = Strongly agree/very often

SEX

1. I get excited when I see _____.   0   1   2   3   4

2. I hug _____.   0   1   2   3   4

3.	I become sexually aroused with _____.	0	1	2	3	4
4.	I caress _____.	0	1	2	3	4
5.	I think about sex with _____.	0	1	2	3	4
6.	I have sexual intercourse with _____.	0	1	2	3	4
7.	I kiss _____.	0	1	2	3	4
8.	I hold hands with _____.	0	1	2	3	4
9.	I think _____ looks sexy.	0	1	2	3	4
10.	I walk with my arm around _____.	0	1	2	3	4

TOTAL _____

DATING

1.	_____ and I share deep secrets with each other.	0	1	2	3	4
2.	_____ and I make each other happy.	0	1	2	3	4
3.	_____ and I understand each other.	0	1	2	3	4
4.	_____ and I like doing things together.	0	1	2	3	4
5.	_____ and I share things together.	0	1	2	3	4
6.	_____ and I make each other feel comfortable.	0	1	2	3	4
7.	_____ and I send notes to each other.	0	1	2	3	4
8.	_____ and I talk about our dreams for the future.	0	1	2	3	4

8

9. _____ and I are good friends. 0 1 2 3 4
10. _____ and I just like to be   0 1 2 3 4
    together.

TOTAL _____

LOVE

1. My relationship with _____ is   0 1 2 3 4
   serious.
2. Nothing will ever keep _____   0 1 2 3 4
   and me apart.
3. I love _____ even if he/she   0 1 2 3 4
   does not return that love.
4. I am engaged to _____ .   0 1 2 3 4
   (Answer either "0" for no or
   "4" for yes.)
5. I have decided to stay with   0 1 2 3 4
   _____ as long as I live.
6. When _____ and I argue,   0 1 2 3 4
   I know that we will work
   things out.
7. I would stay with _____   0 1 2 3 4
   through very difficult times.
8. I have made up my mind to   0 1 2 3 4
   remain true to _____ forever.
9. I love _____ even when   0 1 2 3 4
   he/she embarrasses me.
10. I am married to _____.   0 1 2 3 4
    (Answer either "0" for no
    or "4" for yes.)

TOTAL _____

MAKING YOUR LOVE TRIANGLE

Now that you've carefully read over and honestly rated yourself on the 30 statements, you're ready to score your scale and discover the makeup of your "love triangle." (Let me remind you again that this exercise is for *your* benefit. No one else needs to see the results of your scale.)

The first thing you need to do in scoring the scale is to total the number of points for each of the three categories: sex, dating, and love.

Once you've added up the points for each of the three categories, you will use your totals as the lengths of the three sides of your triangle. For instance, if your total for the sex category was 23, the sex side of your triangle will be 23 units long. If your total for the dating category was 31, the dating side of your triangle will be 31 units long. And if your total for the love category was 22, the love side of your triangle will be 22 units long.

If you have trouble picturing your triangle and would like to visualize it better, you can actually create one. Using a piece of scrap paper, cut out three strips of equal length. Mark on each strip 40 equal units. Label each strip "Sex," "Dating," and "Love." Then, using the totals you got from each category of the scale, cut each strip to its appropriate unit size. Finally, using "Love" as the base of your triangle, "Sex" as the left side, and "Dating" as the right side, tape the strips together to form a triangle, as shown in the following figure.

(Of course, your triangle will have its own size and shape. In fact, one side may be so long that you can't even make a triangle.)

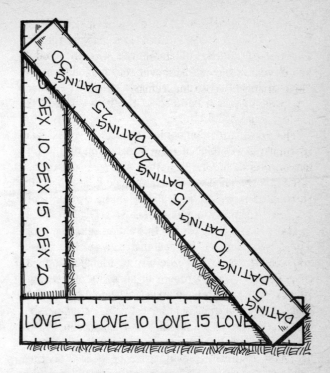

WHAT DOES IT MEAN?

To interpret your triangle, you need to know what the different sides mean.

● *Sex* The left side of your triangle is "sex." We could also call it "eros" (erotic), attachment, or passion. Not much of an explanation is needed here. As mature teenagers, you probably know what it means to be sexually aroused. You're aware of the changes that have taken place in your body during the past few years, and how you respond sexually.

Some relationships are based solely on sex. We can find examples of these without even leaving the first book of the Bible. Potiphar's wife was attracted to Joseph and wanted to have sex with him. Seventeen-year-old Joseph refused, and as a result lost his job and went to prison because of the false charges she made (Genesis 39).

Of course, men sometimes want only sexual relationships as well. Shechem was turned on by Joseph's half sister Dinah. One day when she went out to visit some other women in the neighborhood, he raped her. He wanted sex, and he got it. Then he wanted more and tried to marry her (Genesis 34:1-4).

There is nothing wrong with wanting sex. The problem is getting it outside the marriage relationship. If you're married, the sex side of your triangle should be large because you express your sexuality in marriage. However, if you aren't married, it should be smaller. The less commitment you have to that other person, the smaller the sex side of your triangle should be.

● *Dating* The right side of your triangle is "dating." We could also call it belongingness, "philia," sharing, openness, affection, or friendship. It means being able to share some of your deepest struggles and dreams with that special person. It means being able to talk with him or her at a deeper level than you talk with anyone else.

Of course, dating as a means of courtship is a modern invention, but this special kind of sharing and communication existed even in Old Testament times. An example of it can be found in the relationship between Samson and Delilah.

You know the story. The secret of Samson's

12

strength was a mystery to everyone. Delilah tried again and again to get him to reveal it. Finally, she got him to confide in her, and he told her everything. He talked with her at a deeper level than he had ever talked with anyone other than his parents (Judges 16). This is what is meant by "dating."

The dating side of your triangle will get longer and longer as you share more and more with that special person in your life. Too often people neglect this part of a relationship. As you "go with" another person, you need to increasingly share yourself with him or her.

● *Love* The base of your triangle is "love." We could also call it "agape," caring, decision, or commitment. It means committing yourself to someone and remaining faithful to that commitment. We find the highest level of love in a lasting marriage relationship.

God describes the extent of this love in His Word: "For this reason a man will leave his father and mother and be united to his wife, and they will become one flesh" (Genesis 2:24). This is God's plan to start and maintain new homes. Young men and women leave their parents and begin families of their own.

We find this kind of love on the part of Isaac and Rebekah. Abraham, Isaac's father, had sent his servant to find a wife for his son. When the servant found Rebekah, she and her family agreed to the marriage. Although they often disagreed with each other, especially about rearing their children, Isaac and Rebekah kept this marriage commitment to each other until their deaths.

The love side of your triangle reflects the commitment you've made to that other person. If you've just started dating, the love side will be short; if you're married, it should be long. Unfortunately, life-long commitment is not as popular as it once was in our society.

To better understand the concept of the love triangle, let's examine the triangles of the three couples we met at the beginning of this chapter—Celeste and Frazer, Greta and Forrest, and Linda and Rod.

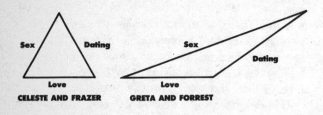

CELESTE AND FRAZER   GRETA AND FORREST

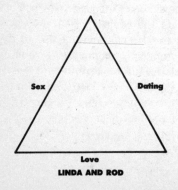

LINDA AND ROD

Notice that, since Celeste and Frazer had only had two dates, all sides of their love triangle are short. They had not had time to let their sides grow. Greta and Forrest's triangle, while larger than Celeste and Frazer's, is out of balance. Notice how much longer the sex side is than the other two sides. This is a result of the emphasis Greta and Forrest place on the *physical* side of their relationship. Linda and Rod's triangle is not only much larger than the other two, it is also well-balanced because of Linda and Rod's decision to make sure all sides of their triangle grow equally. A large part of that decision was their resolution to express their sexuality only within the love commitment of a marriage relationship.

CHANGING TRIANGLES

The triangle you made from the results of the "Sex, Dating, & Love Scale" gives you an idea of how you rate in each of these dimensions of your own romantic relationship. Your triangle, like everyone else's, will constantly change size and shape as time passes. You will become more or less sexually attracted to that other person. You will share more or less with him or her. Your commitment will increase or decrease.

As we discuss sex, dating, and love in the following chapters, you will want to return to this chapter and take the "Sex, Dating, & Love Scale" again and again. You may find that the sides of your triangle should change because one side becomes too long or too short.

2

WHAT HAPPENED TO YOUR BODY?

We were driving home from church one Sunday evening when our son, Keith, was nine years old. He noticed Cliff, a college student, on his way to our house walking with a girl. Keith was very disturbed to see Cliff walking with a girl.

Keith said, "When Cliff gets to our house, I'll have to warn him about girls."

When Cliff and the girl arrived, Keith took him off into a corner and said, "Cliff, you have to watch out for girls. You can get to liking them, and even get married, maybe."

Knowing that Keith was only nine, Cliff solemnly took the warning (giving us a wink)—and walked the girl back to campus at the end of the evening.

When Keith was in high school and college, he walked with girls and started dating them too. What happened? Changes took place in his body—like they have in yours.

A few years ago you guys thought girls were ugly and hated sitting next to them at school. And you girls thought guys were mean and were glad they didn't want to sit near you.

However, all that changed. Suddenly girls began to look good to you guys, and just looking at them would turn you on. Having a guy's arm around you began to feel good to you girls, and you began to get excited too. Knowing about these changes will help you understand yourself.

CHANGES IN YOUR BODY (MOTIVATION) AND SEX

You know about many of the changes that take place in your body around the time of puberty. You grow taller and stronger. Hair appears under your arms and on the pubic area between your legs. Pimples appear on your face. For you guys, your beard begins to grow and your voice cracks. For you girls, your breasts begin to develop and menstrual periods start.

All of you have either experienced these changes or seen them take place in your friends. They are the changes that signal puberty, or sexual maturity. For the first time in your life, you may become pregnant if you're a female, or you may father a child if you're a male.

At the root, these physical changes are changes in your brain and in your glands. The hypothalamus in your brain signaled your pituitary gland to send a hormone to make you grow faster. A little later the same process started your sex glands producing ova and sperm. When that happened, you passed through puberty. You were sexually mature.

These changes in your body bring about changes in your motivation. Before the changes, you had little interest in people of the opposite sex. Now you find yourself attracted to them. You find reasons to be near them.

When these physical changes take place, the sex side of your love triangle may increase. You may become more and more sexually involved with someone. There is nothing wrong with sexual involvement—*as long as the other sides of the triangle are large enough*. That is, sexual intercourse is desirable within the sharing and commitment relationship of marriage. The problem comes when the sexual side of the triangle gets larger while the dating and love sides are still small.

There's no need to spend much time talking about these physical changes and changes in sexual motivation because you already know about them. You know that your sexual desires have increased. What you may not know is that other changes also occurred about the same time, and they influence the other two sides of your triangle.

CHANGES IN YOUR THINKING (COGNITION) AND LOVE

Nadine had just turned 15. Thinking about the future, she said, "Just think, Daddy, in one more year I'll be able to get my driver's license."

"No, you won't," replied her father.

"Why not?" asked Nadine.

"Because I said so."

"That doesn't tell me why not, Dad. I'll be 16. Why can't I get a license?" asked Nadine.

"Because you can't get a license unless I sign for you, and I'm not going to sign."

"But you signed for Bill when he turned 16. Why won't you sign for me?"

"Because you're a girl," replied her father.

"That doesn't make any sense, Dad. Girls are just as able to drive as boys are," said Nadine.

"Not in my book," said her father. "You aren't going to drive until you're 18, and that's that."

Nadine had seen a big change in her parents during the last two or three years. They used to be nice, but now they had become unreasonable. Every time she asked them to explain their reasons for certain things, they gave her such dumb answers. Everyone knew that women could drive as well as men, but her father kept on with the stupid "women driver" jokes. Even though women matured about two years *earlier* than men, her father was serious about her not getting her driver's license until two years *later* than the age her brother got his.

Alex had noticed a change in his parents too. His folks used to be really cool. Suddenly, one Sunday night he realized what they were really like.

"Alex, there's a special on African elephants on 'National Geographic' tonight. After that, there's a special segment on the human arteries on 'Nova,'" said his dad.

"But, Dad, we'll miss the first half of the movie if we watch those shows," protested Alex.

"Alex, the reviews of that movie in today's paper said that it has a lot of bad language and sexual situations in it," said his mother.

"It's not that bad," said Alex. "I watch movies like that all the time."

" 'National Geographic' and 'Nova' will be better for all of us," said his father.

It was then that Alex suddenly realized that his mom and dad weren't cool, beautiful, and handsome. They watched educational TV and listened to public radio. They were more like nerds. He looked at how they were dressed. None of his friends' parents looked that way. Alex's parents looked like geeks.

Real changes had taken place in the families of Nadine and Alex in the past couple of years, but the changes weren't in their parents. The changes were in Nadine and Alex, in how they thought. For the first time in their lives, Nadine and Alex could put together logical arguments and imagine what perfect parents would be like. Their thinking had matured. Psychologists call this cognitive development.

Nadine's parents had *always* used sexist, illogical thinking, but she never realized it. As a child she thought of her mom and dad as perfect and never questioned what they said. Whenever they answered, "Because I said so," that was good enough for her. But now it wasn't good enough. Now whenever she asked for an explanation, she never seemed to get a reasonable answer. Nadine could now think like an adult and see that her parents' reasoning was wrong.

Alex's parents hadn't changed either. They dressed the same way and watched the same programs they had for 20 years. The difference is that now Alex could imagine perfect parents, and he realized that his mom and dad were far from perfect. They couldn't make smart comebacks and were very common people. His church and his town were also not the perfect places he once thought they were.

Modern interest in the way our thinking changes during adolescence began with Swiss psychologist Jean Piaget in the 1920s. He said that at about age 11 or 12, people begin to enter the stage of "formal operations" and begin to be able to think abstractly. They are able to imagine things they have never seen, and things that can't be seen.

As far back as 2,000 years ago people realized that children and adults thought differently. The Apostle Paul wrote, "When I was a child, I talked like a child, I thought like a child, I reasoned like a child. When I became a man, I put childish ways behind me" (1 Corinthians 13:11).

Your thinking has changed too—or will likely change soon. When you solve problems and equations in algebra, chemistry, and computer programming, you are using abstract thinking. As children you were unable to do that kind of thinking. Now you're able to think like adults. Just as your body matures at puberty, so does your mind.

This change in your thinking, known as cognitive development, means that you're able to make the decision to love another person, to commit yourself to him or her. Until you mature in your thinking, your "love" remains at an emotional level, and gets turned off and on whenever you get mad or happy. With this change in your thinking, you can commit yourself to another person for life, and decide to love him or her even when you're angry. The love side of your triangle can grow longer as your thinking matures.

CHANGES IN YOUR FEELINGS (EMOTIONS) AND DATING

As Alex walked in the door around 11:00 one night, his mom looked up from watching the news and said, "Where've you been, Son?"

"Nowhere," Alex replied.

"What have you been doing?" she asked.

"Nothing," said Alex as he walked up the stairs.

Alex knew that she thought he was hiding something from her, but he'd told her the truth. He had just been out walking around the neighborhood alone for the past two hours.

Alex had been trying to figure out life. He just couldn't seem to find where he fit into everything. He didn't feel like he was an adult, but he certainly wasn't a child. He wanted to work, but the law said he had to go to school. He wanted to do something important, but it seemed like he was just not able to.

As he walked that evening, he felt alone—but he often felt that way even when he was with other people. When he was with the guys, he had to be one of them. He couldn't tell them how he really felt. He wondered if any of the other guys felt the same way. He knew that if he told them how he felt inside, they would think he was a jerk. And since he wanted the guys to like him, Alex kept his thoughts to himself.

Nadine had less trouble than Alex in talking with others. When two of her friends had spent the night with her, they all talked until 3:00 in the morning. Then they giggled their way through breakfast the next morning. Then, just after her friends left, Nadine's brother made a smart comment about them, and Nadine burst into tears.

23

"That's why you can't get your driver's license next year, Nadine," said her father. "Teenage girls are just too emotional. If that would happen while you were driving, you could cause an accident."

Although she was really angry, Nadine just bit her lip and turned red, as a tear rolled down her cheek. She knew that if she said anything about being angry, her father would just say that it proved his point. She had been through that before.

Nadine's brother was just as emotional as she was, only he reacted by shouting and throwing things rather than crying. If anything could cause an accident, his temper could. The whole situation made her so depressed that she went into her room and cried quietly. Of course she had feelings, but so did all the other teenagers she knew.

Your emotions are developing just like Nadine's. As your body and your thinking change during puberty and adolescence, they bring about changes in your feelings.

Psychoanalyst Eric Erikson found that during our teen years and into our early twenties, we go through two internal crises. One is the conflict between our identity and our confusion about where we fit into society. Since society does not clearly define where teenagers fit in, many young people do not have a clear sense of identity, of who they are. Erikson calls this the identity crisis. Our society expects us to go out and create our own identity.

The second crisis comes after we've established our identity. This crisis is the conflict between intimacy and isolation. We have to decide whether we will open up and share our deepest thoughts with special other

24

people—or whether we will build walls between ourselves and even our closest friends. Will we be intimate with them—or isolate ourselves from them? If
we don't know who we are, it's difficult to reveal to
others what we really think and feel. We feel isolated,
and the dating side of our triangle is unable to grow.

RESPONSIBILITY IN SEX, DATING, AND LOVE

We've seen that developments during your teen years
in your body, thinking, and feelings affect the three
sides of your triangle—sex, love, and dating. During
this time you become capable of sexual activities, commitment, and sharing—things you could not do as a
child.

One other major development takes place at the
same time, and it affects all three sides of your love
triangle. Harvard psychologist Lawrence Kohlberg followed the lead of Jean Piaget in studying moral development. Both of these men found that during our teen
years we begin to be able to make adult moral judg-
ments.

Consider the following scenarios: Little Johnny was
trying to reach into the cookie jar to get a cookie that
his mother had told him he could not have. While
reaching over the cabinet, he broke a cup. Little Billy
was trying to help his mother by setting the table. As
he walked into the dining room, he tripped and broke
ten cups. Who did the worse thing, Johnny or Billy?

Most *children* will reply that Billy did a worse thing
than Johnny because Billy broke ten cups while Johnny
only broke one. However, most *teenagers* will say that
Johnny did a worse thing because he broke the cup

25

while he was doing something wrong. Even though he broke only one cup, his intention (motivation) was wrong, so he did the worse thing. Once you become a teenager, you can judge a person's motives even though you cannot *see* those motives.

The church has long talked about the "age of ac-countability," or the age at which God holds people responsible for what they do. Many people believe that this happens about the time a person becomes a teenager. They argue that children do not really know the difference between right and wrong; therefore, it makes no sense to hold them responsible until they can make moral decisions like other adults.

Most religious conversions occur around the time of puberty, when a young person begins to realize the difference between right and wrong. At that time in their lives young people realize that they have sinned and feel guilty for what they have done. Then they are faced with the choice of asking for God's forgiveness, or resisting God—the most important decision they will ever make.

As you develop into an adult morally, you become responsible for what you do in sex, dating, and love. When you mature physically so that you can have sex-ual relations, you become responsible for what you do sexually. You are able to sin sexually, and God holds you responsible for what you do with your sexuality.

As you mature in your thinking and are able to make a commitment to other people, God holds you respon-sible for keeping that commitment. When you were younger, you were not able to fully understand what it meant to make a commitment. Now that you do, you must keep it.

As you mature in your feelings, God holds you responsible for how you treat others. Even though you may become angry with others, you must still treat them with respect.

The Apostle Paul best summed up these changes when he said, "Brothers, stop thinking like children. In regard to evil be infants, but in your thinking be adults" (1 Corinthians 14:20).

3

THE INVENTION OF ADOLESCENCE

Jesus was a teenager, but never an adolescent,"
Don Joy said several years ago. I was puzzled.
Adolescence is defined as the period between puberty
and adulthood. I thought teenagers were adolescents,
and adolescents were teenagers.

However, such was not the case. In fact, adolescence is something that has been created in very recent history. To better understand this concept, let's go back in time and look at the lives of young people throughout various stages of history.

MOSES AND MIRIAM: HEBREWS IN AN EGYPTIAN WORLD

Pharaoh's daughter was bathing in the river one day when she noticed a floating basket. She had her servant girl bring the basket to her.

She opened it and saw the baby. He was crying, and she felt sorry for him. "This is one of the Hebrew babies," she said.

Then his [the baby's] sister asked Pharaoh's daughter, "Shall I go and get one of the Hebrew women to nurse the baby for you?"

"Yes, go," she answered. And the girl went and got the baby's mother. Pharaoh's daughter said to her, "Take this baby and nurse him for me, and I will pay you." So the woman took the baby and nursed him. When the child grew older, she took him to Pharaoh's daughter and he became her son. She named him Moses, saying, "I drew him out of the water."

One day, after Moses had grown up, he went out . . . (Exodus 2:6-11).

Was Moses ever an adolescent? Notice that he was called a "baby" six times in the previous passage. When he was a little older, he was called a "child." In the next verse he "had grown up." Moses was a teenager over 3,000 years ago, but was he an adolescent?

Moses and his sister Miriam were Hebrew slaves growing up in an Egyptian culture. Did they ever experience a time between puberty and adulthood? What about sex, dating, and love while they were teenagers? To find out, we need to look at the Talmud, a collection of the oral law of the ancient Hebrews. Of course, we do not know what teachers were alive when Moses and Miriam were teenagers, but here is what some of them might have said.

Some would have told Moses' father, Amram, to lead his children in the right path and marry them "just before they attain puberty" (Sanhedrin 76b). A father was to marry his children just before sexual maturity so that sex and marriage could start about the same time.

In Old Testament times, there was no "dating" like today. The parents usually arranged the marriages of their children. Sometimes the mother did it, such as when Hagar got a wife for Ishmael. "While he was living in the Desert of Paran, his mother got a wife for him from Egypt" (Genesis 21:21). Sometimes the father arranged it, as when Abraham asked his servant to "go to my country and my own relatives and get a wife for my son Isaac" (Genesis 24:4).

Moses and Miriam lived about 3,000 years ago as Hebrew slaves in Egypt. They were teenagers, but they were never adolescents like you. Sexual activity began at puberty, but within the commitment of a marriage relationship. Dating, along with the rest of adolescence, had not been "invented" yet. Love triangles of teenagers in Moses' and Miriam's time would look like this:

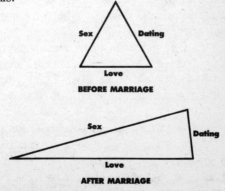

Sex / Dating

Love

BEFORE MARRIAGE

Sex / Dating

Love

AFTER MARRIAGE

Next, let's examine teenagers of New Testament times—approximately 2,000 years ago.

PAUL AND PRISCILLA: JEWS IN A GREEK AND ROMAN WORLD

Writing to people in Corinth, a city in Greece, Paul said, "When I was a child, I talked like a child, I thought like a child, I reasoned like a child. When I became a man, I put childish ways behind me" (1 Corinthians 13:11). Paul talks about being a child (four times in one verse), then about being a man. He never mentions being an adolescent.

As a Roman citizen (Acts 22:27-28), Paul could have married when he was 14. Of course, he probably would not have married quite that early since puberty for most men then occurred around the age of 17 or 18, like in Moses' time.

We do not know the name of Paul's sister (Acts 23:16), but let's call her Priscilla. As Roman citizens, her parents would have begun to look for a husband for Priscilla when she turned 13. If she were still unmarried at 19, Priscilla would have been considered an old maid.

Marriages during Roman times were generally arranged by parents or by professional "marriage-brokers"—so dating did not exist 2,000 years ago either. In fact, Latin had no word that could be translated as "date."

The lowest legal age for marriage under Roman law was 12 for women and 14 for men. As was the case 1,000 years earlier, sexual activity could begin at puberty within the relationship of marriage. The creation of dating was still nearly 2,000 years in the future.

Love triangles of teenagers in Paul and Priscilla's time would look like those in Moses and Miriam's time. Little had changed in the development of adolescence since Moses and Miriam's time.

Let's move on and examine teenagers of 1,000 years ago in medieval England.

EDWARD AND ELIZABETH: ANGLO-SAXONS

Let's imagine a medieval English family with two children, Edward and Elizabeth. Edward and Elizabeth's parents could arrange their marriages when they were as young as seven. Either the parents or the children could call off the marriage until Edward or Elizabeth was ten with no penalty. That gave the parents two or three years to change their minds if they thought the marriage partners they had chosen were wrong for Edward or Elizabeth.

If Edward or Elizabeth were between the ages of 10 and 12, the parents could be fined for calling off the marriage. Between ages 10 and 12, Edward and Elizabeth themselves could call off the marriage if they wanted to. However, after Edward or Elizabeth turned 12, both the parents and the child could be fined if they called off the wedding.

In England, as in Rome, the earliest age that men could marry without permission from their parents was 14, and the earliest age women could marry was 12. Again, sexual activity would begin within the marriage relationship.

The love triangles of teenagers 1,000 years ago would be the same as those in Hebrew and Roman times. Little had changed in 2,000 years.

33

Now let us continue our journey through time, moving from England of 1,000 years ago to colonial America, only 200 years ago.

MICHAEL AND MARTHA: COLONIAL AMERICANS

Let's imagine Michael and Martha, a Puritan brother and sister. Their father would probably see that they were married at puberty. The Puritans thought that the best way to keep their teenage sons and daughters sexually pure was to see that they married as soon as possible after they became sexually mature. They disagreed with the Catholics of the time who, the Puritans believed, "ensnared" their children in "vows of virginity."

As Puritan Thomas Cobett put it, celibate young people would "not be able to contain" and would be involved in "unnatural pollutions, and other filthy practices in secret: and too oft of horrid Murthers of the fruit of their bodies." (They would have sex before marriage and get pregnant.) The sexual maturity of puberty came at about the same time as the love and commitment of marriage.

The love triangles of teenage Americans 200 years ago would be like those of the Hebrews, Romans, and Anglo-Saxons. Little had changed in nearly 3,000 years of history.

Michael and Martha living 200 years ago in America were teenagers, but never adolescents like you. Like people throughout 3,000 years of history before them, they went directly from childhood to adulthood without any adolescence. Sexual maturity and marriage came at about the same time.

JOHN AND JANE: MODERN AMERICANS

Now in our journey through time, let's move up to the present and discover the beginnings of adolescence. Two things have happened in recent history to bring about adolescence.

First, the age of puberty has decreased. Between 1800 and 1880, scientists conducted 64 separate studies on women, asking them when they had their first menstrual period (an event closely associated with the beginning of puberty). Not a single study found the average age *below* 14.5 years. The overall average was about 16. Between 1960 and 1980, scientists conducted 24 similar studies, and only one of them found an average *above* 14.5 years. Jane, a typical American female, would likely go through puberty between ages 12 and 13, rather than at 16 as Miriam, Priscilla, Elizabeth, and Martha probably did.

Today, John, a typical American male, would most likely become sexually mature at about age 14, rather than at 17 or 18 as Moses, Paul, Edward, and Michael probably did.

Second, the age at which people become adults has changed. After 3,000 years of recognizing people as adults and allowing them to marry at age 12 or 14, today people are not recognized as adults until they are at least 18. Today John and Jane could not work or marry in most states until they are 18. They are treated as children, even though they are adults in both their bodies and in their thinking.

Since adolescence is the time in our lives between puberty and adulthood, for the first time in history we have adolescents.

Love triangles of today, as shown in the following figure, are quite different from those of teenagers in the past. Since teens today cannot legally make the commitment of love in marriage, the bases of their triangles must be short. Those who are not dating have all sides short, like unmarried teens in the past. However, some dating teens have both the sex and dating sides long. Still others have only the sex side long. Whenever the sides get out of proportion, a problem may develop since it is not a full relationship.

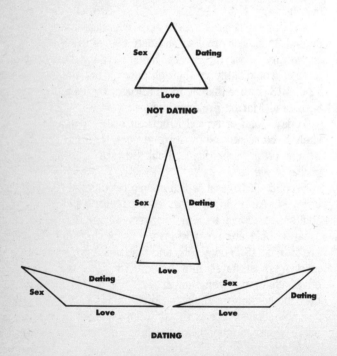

JUST WHO ARE THE CRAZY ONES?

A friend of mine defines adolescence as "a period of temporary insanity between childhood and adulthood." He's right! But it's not teenagers who are crazy. It's society. Society recognizes you as children and treats you like children, while telling you you should act like adults.

Older adults may think you're crazy, but how else can you act in such a crazy world? You want to be adults, but people won't let you.

Sometimes you yourself might think you're crazy. After all, why else would you have sexual desires before you can marry? Why else would you feel the way you do? Why else would you think the way you do? Of course, the truth is that any other adult would act a little crazy if he or she had to live with the same restrictions that you do.

The invention of adolescence has influenced sex, dating, and love. Before the invention of adolescence, people were able to marry when they reached puberty. Sexual maturity and marriage could occur at about the same time. (Of course, not everyone married when he or she reached 12 or 14, just as everyone does not marry when he or she reaches 18 now. The point is that they were not forced to remain single if they wanted to marry.)

The fact that today people mature sexually at 12 or 14 and cannot marry until they are at least 18 has led to more sexual activity among unmarried teenagers. And of course this increased sexual activity affects the sex side of your triangle. (We will discuss this effect in more detail in chapters 4, 5, and 6.)

Dating did not even exist until adolescence was in-

vented during this past century. With parents no longer choosing mates, teenagers had to have some way
of picking the person they wanted to live with for the
rest of their lives. Obviously, this affects the dating
side of the triangle. (We will discuss this effect in
more detail in chapters 7, 8, and 9.)

The commitment of love in a marriage relationship
is not even allowed to you as a teenager today. You
cannot marry until you are at least 18. Even if you
could marry, other laws and customs would keep you
from earning enough money to live. This affects the
love side of your triangle. (We will discuss this effect
in more detail in chapters 10, 11, and 12.)

The Hebrews, Romans, Anglo-Saxons, and Puritans
did not have all the answers. How would you like to
marry someone your parents picked out, but you hardly knew? There was no chance for sharing to develop
between a couple in a dating relationship. Unfortunately,
our system is not perfect either. Most teens become
sexually active before they marry, and the dating side
of their triangle still does not grow. Therefore, the
rest of this book is designed to help you cause all the
sides of your love triangle to grow at the same time.

4

HOW FAR IS TOO FAR?

Friday night Randy and Ann rented a video to watch at Randy's house while his parents were at a Sunday School party. As they cuddled closer on the couch, Ann could feel Randy's hands caressing her body. She tried to move away, but he kept pulling her closer. Finally, she said, "Don't, Randy. I don't want to go too far."

"Why not?" asked 16-year-old Randy. "You turn me on, and I feel like having sex."

"I'm excited too," said 15-year-old Ann. "But I don't think I'm ready for sex."

"Let's do it tonight," said Randy. "We've been dating a month and I love you."

"I don't know," said Ann. "It's one thing to talk about it, but it's another thing to do it."

"Don't you love me?" asked Randy.

"You know I do," Ann replied.

"Then show me."

"I don't know," replied Ann. "I've always heard you shouldn't have sex before marriage."

"Why not?" asked Randy.

"Because I might get pregnant. What would I do then?"

"You don't have to worry about that," said Randy. "There are lots of kinds of birth control."

"I've read about it and talked about it, but I've never done it before," said Ann. "I'm not sure I'd know what to do."

"Don't worry about that," replied Randy. "I've done it with several girls. I'll show you what to do."

"You've done it with several girls! What am I—just another one on your list? What if you caught something from one of those girls and then I caught it from you? There are lots of diseases people get from having sex," she said.

"They were all nice girls and I'm sure they didn't have anything," replied Randy. "But just to be sure, we can have safe sex. You won't get pregnant and you can't catch anything."

"But isn't it wrong?" asked Ann. "People at church always say you should have sex only after you're married."

"That's just an old-fashioned idea," replied Randy. "Those people grew up in a time when most people waited. Get with it, Ann. This is the twentieth century."

"The Bible says that it's wrong," said Ann. "One of the Ten Commandments is 'You shall not commit adultery.' "

"You have to be married to commit adultery. We're not married, so we can't commit adultery."

"Everything you say seems to make sense," Ann said, "but it still doesn't seem right to me. I need to think about it some more."

"Well, at least we can pet. You don't have anything against that, do you?" asked Randy.

"Well, I like holding your hand, and having your arm around me," said Ann. "What else do you want to do?"

"I want to touch every part of your body and have you touch every part of mine. That feels almost as good as going all the way," Randy said.

"I don't think so, Randy," replied Ann. "I want to save my body for my husband after I'm married."

EXCUSES, EXCUSES

If we were to draw love triangles based on Randy's and Ann's ideas of a relationship, they would probably look something like the following figures:

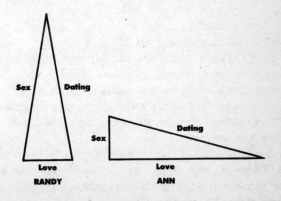

43

Notice how Randy's emphasis is on the sex and dating sides of the triangle, while Ann's emphasis is on the love and dating sides.

As a teenager, you face the same decisions that Randy and Ann faced. Both Randy and Ann were right in many of the things they said. However, they were also wrong in some. Let's take a look at this issue of sex before marriage.

First, Randy suggested that they should have sex because they were in love and had been dating for a month. Of course, he had confused love and sex. Both are part of our relationships, but like many teenage men, he wanted to get on to sex right away.

In *Teenage Sexuality* (Macmillan), Arnold Haas asked hundreds of 15–19-year-old men to finish this statement: "If I went out with a girl, I would want to have sexual intercourse with her . . ." One third of the men said within the first two weeks of dating. Half of the men said within the first month of dating. Love—commitment to that other person—would have little time to grow in only a month.

Second, Ann said they should not have intercourse because she could get pregnant. Randy said many methods of birth control are available. He's right. So is she, because each method has its failure rate—the percentage of women who become pregnant each year while using it. The failure rates vary among the different methods, but none are zero. There is *always* a chance of pregnancy.

Third, Ann raised the problem of sexually transmitted diseases. She is right to think of these, because the number of reported cases is on the rise, and the diseases are becoming more serious. Randy is right in

44

saying that some things make sex *safer,* but there is no such thing as totally "safe sex" outside of marriage. There is always the chance of disease, no matter how nice the other person is and no matter what precautions you take before intercourse.

IS IT WRONG?

Finally, Ann brought up the idea of the Bible saying that premarital sex is wrong. Although the Bible says much about adultery after marriage, it says surprisingly little about sex before marriage. Of course, sex before marriage was not much of a problem in Bible times when people could marry at the age of puberty, when they became sexually mature. You will not find a command about sex before marriage in the Ten Commandments, just as you will not find a command about speed limits for cars on interstate highways. Adolescence and cars are both recent inventions.

However, premarital sex is mentioned several times relating to specific individuals, and is condemned whenever it is mentioned. When Potiphar's wife wanted to have sex with Joseph, it would have been adultery for her, but not for him. He was an unmarried young man. Joseph said, "How then could I do such a wicked thing and sin against God?" (Genesis 39:9) It would have been a sin for him, not just for her.

When the Law was given, it had some commands about virginity at marriage. If a man married a woman who was not a virgin, according to the Law, "She shall be brought to the door of her father's house and there the men of her town shall stone her to death. She has done a disgraceful thing in Israel by being promiscuous while still in her father's house. You must purge the evil from among you" (Deuteronomy 22:21).

The New Testament also addresses the issue of sex before marriage. "Marriage should be honored by all, and the marriage bed kept pure, for God will judge the adulterer and all the sexually immoral" (Hebrews 13:4). The word for the "sexually immoral" is *pornos,* (root of "pornography") a general word for illicit sex, sometimes including adultery. Of course, here it is referring to illicit sex other than adultery.

The church at Corinth was having trouble with the issue of sex among the unmarried. Paul wrote, "But since there is so much immorality, each man should have his own wife, and each woman her own husband" (1 Corinthians 7:2). The way to handle the problem of premarital sex was to marry. (Of course, back then teens could marry.)

The idea that premarital sex is wrong is not popular in the United States today. In 1985 a Roper Poll (*U.S. News & World Report,* 12/9/85) found that only 20 percent of the people 18–29 years old surveyed answered "Yes" to the question, "Is it wrong for a man and a woman to have sexual relations before marriage?" In addition, only 25 percent of the people 30–44 years old, the parents of teenagers, said it was wrong.

Of course, mass opinion does not make premarital sex right. We may live in a democracy where many things are decided by vote, but God does not determine what is sin and what isn't by a majority vote of the American public. Whenever premarital sex is mentioned in the Bible, it is clearly portrayed as being wrong. Therefore, we can conclude that premarital sex is not acceptable to God.

WHAT ABOUT PETTING?

Although the Bible talks about many sexual activities, it does not mention anything about petting as a part of dating. Of course, dating had not been invented then.

The closest the Bible comes to talking about petting is when Isaac and Rebekah were living among the Philistines. Isaac had Rebekah say that she was his sister because he was afraid the Philistines would kill him for her. "When Isaac had been there a long time, Abimelech king of the Philistines looked down from a window and saw Isaac caressing his wife Rebekah. So Abimelech summoned Isaac and said, 'She is really your wife!' " (Genesis 26:8-9)

Notice that the first thing Abimelech thought when he saw them petting (caressing) was that Rebekah was Isaac's wife. It never occurred to him that she might be his girlfriend. When people petted, it meant that they were married. It was something that led to sexual intercourse back then—and often it still does today.

You need to decide how far you are going to go before you date, and hold to that decision while on a date. One rule of thumb I often tell teenagers is, "If it is a part of the body that is covered by a modest swimming suit, keep your hands off."

SEX WITH SAME-SEX FRIENDS

Pat and Lynn have been friends since they were nine years old. One night they were studying together for an English test. Since it was late, Pat invited Lynn to spend the night.

Lying in Pat's big double bed, they stayed up late talking to each other. They had both just gone through

47

puberty, and the subject of sex came up.

Lynn said, "Pat, let's touch each other all over. I did it with someone else last week and it feels great."

"I don't know," said Pat. "Would that be right?"

"Why not?" asked Lynn. "It's not like either one of us can get pregnant from it."

"Wouldn't that make us homosexuals?"

"Just one time wouldn't," replied Lynn.

"But isn't it wrong?"

"People used to think so," said Lynn. "But not any more. Haven't you heard about gay liberation and homosexuals coming out of the closet?"

It is estimated that 25 percent of all men and 10 percent of all women have a homosexual experience at some time in their lives. However, only 4 percent of the men and 2 percent of the women become exclusive homosexuals.

If people have homosexual experiences, they are most likely to have them while teenagers. This is especially true for men. Most of these teens do not go on to become lifelong homosexuals, but does that mean there's nothing wrong with experimenting with homosexuality?

Of course, pregnancy is not an issue, but disease is. One can catch sexually transmitted diseases through homosexual activity just as he or she can through heterosexual activity. However, the possibility of disease is not the only reason to avoid it. Both the Old Testament and the New Testament say that homosexual activity is wrong.

"'If a man lies with a man as one lies with a woman, both of them have done what is detestable. They must be put to death; their blood will be on their own heads' " (Leviticus 20:13).

Because of this, God gave them over to shameful lusts. Even their women exchanged natural relations for unnatural ones. In the same way the men also abandoned natural relations with women and were inflamed with lust for one another. Men committed indecent acts with other men, and received in themselves the due penalty for their perversion (Romans 1:26-27).

Do you not know that the wicked will not inherit the kingdom of God? Do not be deceived: Neither the sexually immoral nor idolaters nor adulterers nor male prostitutes nor homosexual offenders . . . will inherit the kingdom of God (1 Corinthians 6:9).

As with premarital sex, attitudes toward homosexual behavior are changing. In the past, homosexuality was considered sinful, criminal, and a type of mental illness. However, few laws remain making it criminal, and since the 1970s it has not been considered a mental illness. Of course, again, God does not decide what is sinful and what is not by a majority vote.

THE ULTIMATE AUTHORITY

There are many reasons to wait and have sex only in a marriage relationship. Josh McDowell and Dick Day called their book *Why Wait?* and have whole chapters on physical reasons, spiritual reasons, emotional reasons, and relational reasons to wait.

When the Bible talks about not having sex outside the marriage relationship, the major reason given is that God wants us to be holy like Him. This connection between sexual purity and being holy is made clear in 1 Thessalonians 4:3-8:

It is God's will that you should be holy; that you should avoid sexual immorality; that each of you should learn to control his own body in a way that is holy and honorable, not in passionate lust like the heathen, who do not know God; and that in this matter no one should wrong his brother or take advantage of him. The Lord will punish men for all such sins, as we have already told you and warned you. For God did not call us to be impure, but to live a holy life. Therefore, he who rejects this instruction does not reject man but God, who gives you His Holy Spirit.

We often refer to the fact that our bodies are the "temples of God" when encouraging people to eat good foods, exercise, and avoid drugs that harm their bodies. The following passage also relates to this principle.

Flee from sexual immorality. All other sins a man commits are outside his body, but he who sins sexually sins against his own body. Do you not know that your body is a temple of the Holy Spirit, who is in you, whom you have received from God? You are not your own; you were bought at a price. Therefore honor God with your body (1 Corinthians 6:18-20).

The emphasis in this chapter has been on avoiding sinful sexual activity. I realize that many of you reading this book may already be involved in such activity. You need to know that the message of the Bible is one of forgiveness. This is best expressed as "If we confess our sins, He is faithful and just and will forgive us our sins and purify us from all unrighteousness" (1 John 1:9).

God forgives sexual sins, as well as others. We see this when the religious leaders brought a woman caught in the act of adultery to Jesus. They pointed out that under Old Testament law they should stone her, and asked Jesus what He thought. Jesus told anyone who had never sinned to throw the first stone, and they all walked away.

> Jesus straightened up and asked her, "Woman, where are they? Has no one condemned you?"
> "No one, sir," she said.
> "Then neither do I condemn you," Jesus declared. "Go now and leave your life of sin" (John 8:10-11).

Jesus addressed the fact that she had sinned, told her that He forgave her sin, and commanded her to quit sinning. God will forgive your sexual sin, but then He expects you to stop.

5

SEX ALONE

Now that adolescence has been invented, what are you, as a teenager, supposed to do with your sexuality? What about those of you who have already become involved sexually with someone else? Should you just instantly become a nonsexual person? What about masturbation? Since you are not allowed to get married until you're 18, and since sex with someone else before marriage is wrong, what about sex by yourself?

Sean was about 19 and described his sexual life like this: "I used to have 'wet dreams' all the time. I would wake up after them, be all messy, and have trouble getting back to sleep. Now every couple days I look at some sexy pictures in magazines—nothing kinky—and masturbate. I'm able to sleep a lot better now."

Sean's sexual behavior is quite typical of most teenage men, and many teenage women. Is masturbation wrong? In examining this question, we must look at three specific aspects of solo sex: wet dreams, fantasies, and the physical act of masturbation.

WET DREAMS

Like Sean, most young men who are not having sexual intercourse regularly experience sexual orgasms in their sleep. This also occurs with young women, but not quite as often. While asleep, the person becomes sexually aroused and experiences a sexual orgasm. Of course, with young men semen is emitted from the penis, so it is called a "wet dream." Sometimes the person wakes up during the "nocturnal emission" (as wet dreams are technically called), other times he does not.

In the past, some Christians thought that people who experienced nocturnal emissions were sinning. They believed that these people were actually having sex in their sleep. So if an unmarried person had a nocturnal emission, some Christians believed that it must be immorality. They used Deuteronomy 23:10-11 to prove their point. "If one of your men is unclean because of a nocturnal emission, he is to go outside the camp and stay there. But as evening approaches he is to wash himself, and at sunset he may return to the camp."

However, it must be pointed out that, for the ancient Jews, being unclean did not mean being sinful. It meant that the person was *ceremonially* unclean, not allowed to take part in religious ceremonies. Jewish men could become unclean by touching a dead body, a reptile, a woman during her menstrual period, or even something a menstruating woman had sat on (Leviticus 22:4-7; 15:19-23).

Deuteronomy 23:10-11 is the only biblical passage that clearly talks about orgasms in our sleep. A few other verses may be referring to them, but it is not clear that they are. Since people during Old Testament times often married at puberty, apparently nocturnal emissions rarely occurred. And when they did occur, they were of little concern.

I could say that you have to decide for yourself about nocturnal emissions, but that would be foolish. You can't decide whether or not to have them. You can't simply go to bed and say, "I'm not going to have a wet dream tonight."

What you do have to decide about wet dreams is how you feel about them. Most people see nocturnal emissions as a sign of sexual maturity, not a sign of sexual sin. As a teenager today, you have them because you have passed puberty and are not having regular sexual relations in marriage yet.

FANTASIES

Sean, the young man I referred to earlier in the chapter, is like most other teenagers in that he looks at sexy pictures to start sexy thoughts. While this practice has become more "acceptable" in recent years, sexual fantasy has been occurring in both men and women for thousands of years.

More than 50 years ago, before magazines like *Playboy* or *Playgirl* could be bought at the local convenience store and before X-rated movies were available on videotape and on cable TV, Laurance Shaffer and Edward Shoben (*The Psychology of Adjustment,*

Houghton Mifflin) asked 200 college students about their fantasies. Nearly all of them (97 percent of the men and 96 percent of the women) reported having sexual fantasies at some time and about three-fourths (74 percent of the men and 73 percent of the women) reported having them recently.

As a teenager, why do you have sexual fantasies? One reason is that you can't have sexual intercourse. You daydream about things you want but can't have.

You probably don't daydream about food because you can have all you want. During World War II a group of young men were placed on a semi-starvation diet for six months. Before long, the conversations of the men began to center on food. They put up pictures of food in place of sexy pinups. They began reading cookbooks for fun! They wanted food but could not have it, so they thought about little else.

Because you've passed puberty, you are sexually mature. And since you can't marry and have sexual intercourse, you probably daydream about sex. Like the men who were hungry, you fantasize about what you want but can't have.

Is adolescent sexual fantasy wrong? Since adolescence did not exist when the Bible was written, the Bible does not talk specifically about it. However, the Bible does talk about sexual fantasy in adults.

The most often quoted verse dealing with this issue is Matthew 5:28, in which Jesus says, "But I tell you that anyone who looks at a woman lustfully has already committed adultery with her in his heart." Of course, He was talking about adultery, not premarital sex. He was talking about sexual fantasy by married adults, not by unmarried adolescents.

The word translated "lustfully" means "strong desire." In fact, it is often simply translated "desire." For example, Jesus used the same word referring to Himself when He said, "I have eagerly desired to eat this Passover with you before I suffer" (Luke 22:15). The verse in Matthew does not say that if you happen to have a sexual thought when looking at another person you have committed adultery. It does mean that you are not to strongly desire someone who is not your mate.

- *Fantasy Is Forever*

One thing you should know regarding sexual fantasies, though, is that most memories last forever. You may not believe it when you are struggling to answer a question on a test, but it's true. The information is there, you just can't get it out without the right cue. If someone would just give you a hint, the answer would come right out.

The same is true of sexual memories you put into your mind during your teen years. Mike, in his mid-twenties, has been married about a year. He said, "When I was a teenager, my father had pornographic magazines around all the time, so I looked at them. I became a Christian and thought all those memories were gone, but they aren't. When I make love to my wife, all those pictures come back, and I can't concentrate on my love for my wife." The things you are daydreaming about now will be in your mind as long as you live, so be careful what you put there.

- *Pornography*

Pornography is someone else's fantasy; it's not real life. Real people do not look or act like the people you see in magazines, read about in books, or watch in movies. Experimenting with pornography may cause you to develop wrong ideas about sex, and be disappointed in what real people are like. Participants in an experiment at Arizona State University found that they felt less love for their mates and rated them less attractive sexually after they looked at nude pictures from *Playboy* or *Playgirl*.

Pornography gets old quickly. A picture, book, or movie that arouses you sexually when you first see it loses its appeal in a few days. That's why magazines publish a new issue every month and video stores get new X-rated movies every few days. Each time you see pornographic material, you get less excited. Living this fantasy life as an adolescent, you are not preparing for marriage to one person for life, but for needing a new sexual stimulus often.

MASTURBATION

"Woe to them that devise iniquity, and work evil upon their beds! when the morning is light, they practise it, because it is in the power of their hand" (Micah 2:1, KJV). Because of the wording of the King James Version in this verse, some people believe it is referring to masturbation—sexually stimulating yourself. However, if you read this verse in a recent translation, you will find that it is actually talking about plotting evil during the night and performing it during the day.

Nineteen out of 20 teenage men and 2 out of 3 teenage women masturbate. That makes it the most common sexual practice among adolescents today. Before the invention of adolescence, many people believed that masturbation caused nearly every affliction from pimples to insanity. However, by the middle of this century, not only had those myths been proved wrong, but many people were actually *encouraging* teenagers to masturbate.

You may wonder why so many people masturbate. With the invention of adolescence, teenagers began to look for sexual outlets outside of marriage. Masturbation has been around for thousands of years, but during the last century it became "a normal part of growing up." It has become "normal" because teenage marriage became impossible.

Of course, your question is, "Should I or shouldn't I?" To make that decision, you'll need some information.

First, what does the Bible say about it? Nothing. Several verses in the old King James English (such as Micah 2:1) seem to refer to it, but recent translators agree that the Bible does not mention it. That's not much help, is it?

Second, what do Christians say about it? Everything. Some Christians believe it is bad. In *The Christian Counselor's Manual* (Baker), Jay Adams has a chapter section entitled "Masturbation Is Sin." Other Christians believe it is good. In *The Stork Is Dead* (Word), Charlie Shedd has a chapter entitled "Masturbation—Gift of God." That's not much help either, is it?

Third, will it make you sick? Not physically, at least. Masturbation does not cause acne, cancer, or heart trouble. You can't catch any sexually transmitted diseases from yourself. You can't become pregnant (or get someone else pregnant) by yourself.

So if masturbation feels good, if it won't make you sick, if Christians can't agree on it, and if the Bible doesn't say it is wrong, why is it a problem?

Most people see two problems that may develop from masturbation. One is that when some people masturbate, they fantasize—and earlier in the chapter we saw the problems that come with sexual fantasy.

The other problem is that some people withdraw from being with others socially and try to satisfy their needs for love and dating by themselves, through masturbation. Even before sin entered the world, "The Lord God said, 'It is not good for the man to be alone. I will make a helper suitable for him' " (Genesis 2:18). People were created with needs for communication and commitment.

Masturbation is not the way God intended for you to express your sexuality. It is just sex without any love or dating. With it you have no commitment to or sharing with another person. In fact, another person is not even involved. This is not to say that masturbation is evil, just that it is not best.

A LIFE OF FRUSTRATION?

You may ask, "Does God mean for me to live in sexual frustration?" The answer to that is no! Our culture is what causes you to live in frustration. God meant for us to live our sexual lives fully.

To some people that means never marrying and experiencing sexual intercourse. To them, celibacy (remaining single) is good.

It is good for a man not to marry (1 Corinthians 7:1).

Now to the unmarried and the widows I say: It is

good for them to stay unmarried, as I am
(1 Corinthians 7:8).

Some of you don't have strong sexual drives and
you wonder what all the fuss is about in not being able
to have sex. For you, living unmarried is good.

To other people, living their sexual lives fully means
having sexual relations within marriage.

But since there is so much immorality, each man
should have his own wife, and each woman her
own husband (1 Corinthians 7:2).

But if they cannot control themselves, they
should marry, for it is better to marry than to
burn with passion (1 Corinthians 7:9).

God is certainly not responsible for sexual frustrations. The message of the Bible is to express our
sexuality in marriage. Our culture invented adolescence with its sexual frustrations. We must make sure
we don't blame God for what our society has done.

SEX IN A FALLEN WORLD

You're probably saying, "We still haven't answered the
basic question: What do we do with our sexuality?"
You're right. This is the most difficult question of adolescence, and there is no good answer to it.

We have seen that God intended for us to marry
and make the sex side of our triangle larger within the
commitment of marriage. Our culture passed laws
making it illegal for us to do that. (Changing laws about
the minimum legal age of marriage would do little good

because there are still laws making you go to school and keeping you from working.)

This means that the sexual side of your love triangles can't be all that God intended while you are teenagers. Since sex with others is sinful and dangerous, your choice is to live in frustration or have sex alone. Don't think there is something wrong with you or blame God for it. The problem is a culture developed in a sinful world.

6

STD's—SOMETHING OLD AND SOMETHING NEW

The name is new, but the idea is old—STD.
STD stands for Sexually Transmitted Diseases,
the new name for what your parents called venereal
diseases, or VD. (Venus was the Roman goddess of
love, so "venereal" referred to sexual intercourse.)
Today rather than calling these diseases "venereal,"
we come right out and say that they are "sexually
transmitted."

In the 1940s, people thought sexually transmitted
diseases were a thing of the past. Today they are in
the headlines almost daily. We can't talk about the
sexual side of our love triangle without discussing sexually transmitted diseases. Although many sexually
transmitted diseases exist, let's take a close look at
five of the major ones: syphilis, gonorrhea, chlamydia,
herpes, and AIDS.

THE IMITATOR

As 17-year-old Crystal was taking a shower, she noticed a hard, round bump, about the size of a dime, between her legs on her genitals. Since it did not hurt or itch or burn, Crystal assumed she must have bumped herself there. She did nothing about it and in a few weeks it went away, leaving a flat, smooth, pale spot on her skin.

Crystal had just missed her first chance to stop the damage taking place in her body.

A couple months later, she developed a skin rash, some sores in her mouth, and ran a low fever with general aches and pains. Crystal assumed she had the flu or was allergic to something. Again the symptoms went away.

Crystal had just missed her second chance to stop the damage.

Crystal had syphilis, "the great imitator," and had just gone through the primary and secondary stages of the disease. It is called the great imitator because the early symptoms are often mistaken for other illnesses. When this happens, syphilis is usually left untreated because the symptoms, like those of less serious diseases, go away by themselves.

However, syphilis is different; the disappearance of symptoms does not mean the disease is cured, but that it has entered a latent (hidden) stage. During the next few years Crystal will have no more *noticeable* symptoms, but the "spirochetes" (the organisms that cause syphilis) will silently attack some part or parts of her body. They may attack the circulatory system, causing Crystal's heart to become overworked and enlarged, eventually causing heart failure. They may attack the nervous system so that she becomes unco-ordinated, has odd sensations, loses some of her reflexes, or becomes mentally ill. These internal effects may not happen for 10, 20, or even 30 years.

Syphilis is "something old." People argue about when and where it originated. Some people believe it has been around since Old Testament times, and that the following passage in Deuteronomy is a description of its stages:

> The Lord will afflict you with the boils of Egypt and with tumors, festering sores and the itch, from which you cannot be cured. The Lord will afflict you with madness, blindness and confusion of mind. At midday you will grope about like a blind man in the dark. You will be unsuccessful in everything you do; day after day you will be oppressed and robbed, with no one to rescue you (Deuteronomy 28:27-29).

Of course, no biblical passage can *prove* the existence of syphilis then. Remember, syphilis is the great imitator, and even today is often mistaken for other diseases.

Other people believe syphilis originated in the Americas and was carried to Europe by Columbus and his men. In 1495, a terrible plague of syphilis broke out, and by 1500 it had spread throughout Europe. It is truly "something old."

If Crystal had lived before the 1940s, nothing could have been done to cure her disease. However, in the 1940s, doctors discovered penicillin, which, in one dose, will cure most syphilis. Even though syphilis could be wiped out if everyone who has it were treated with penicillin, doctors report (as they are required to do by law) more than 70,000 new cases every year—and that figure is increasing in the 1980s.

We have talked about symptoms, results, and the cure for syphilis, but not about how it is transmitted. Crystal did not catch it from a toilet seat, bathtub, or doorknob. The spirochetes cannot live outside the body, so syphilis must be passed from person to person by touching the mucous membranes (moist inner surfaces) of the genital tracts. In other words, the only way to catch syphilis is through sexual contact with someone who has the disease.

Before ending our discussion of syphilis, it must be emphasized that a blood test is the only sure diagnosis of the disease, and only penicillin given *for syphilis* can cure it. If Crystal thinks that the penicillin she took for strep throat will cure her syphilis, she is wrong. Penicillin for strep throat is usually given in pills in small dosages over several days. Penicillin for syphilis must be given in one massive dose, by injection. Taking penicillin for another disease will not cure syphilis.

THE STERILIZER

When 17-year-old Brian urinated, he noticed itching and pain. Soon a pus-like substance began to drip from his penis. The pain and burning sensation hurt so much that he went to the doctor to see what was wrong. Brian discovered that he had gonorrhea.

Brian was more fortunate than most women who get gonorrhea. When a woman gets it, she often has no symptoms. She simply thinks that the pus-like discharge, if it occurs, is normal. If untreated in either men or women, the initial symptoms disappear, but the bacteria causing the disease continue to work their way up the genital tract.

Since the symptoms are so obvious in men, most men, like Brian, are treated before the disease becomes the "sterilizer." However, since women have few symptoms, the gonorrhea bacteria often reach the fallopian tubes and the ovaries where they cause sterility. Thus, women may not be able to have children even after the gonorrhea is cured.

Like syphilis, gonorrhea is "something old." References in ancient Egyptian, Hebrew, Greek, and Chinese writings indicate that it existed thousands of years ago. This is probably what is referred to in Leviticus 15:2-3, 25:

"Speak to the Israelites and say to them: 'When any man has a bodily discharge, the discharge is unclean. Whether it continues flowing from his body or is blocked, it will make him unclean. . . .When a woman has a discharge of blood for many days at a time other than her monthly period or has a discharge that continues beyond her period, she will be unclean as long as she has the discharge, just as in the days of her period.' "

Also like syphilis, gonorrhea can be treated with penicillin. Again, it must be of a specific dose, and may require other drugs if a resistant strain is caught. Brian cannot count on penicillin taken for some other disease for a cure. Furthermore, he must inform everyone with whom he has had sexual contact of his disease (remember, women usually have no symptoms).

Unlike syphilis, gonorrhea has not become less common since a cure for it was found. In fact, it has become so common that scientists say it occurs more often than any other communicable disease except the common cold. Doctors are also required to report gonorrhea, and they report about a million cases a year—four times as many as chicken pox.

Gonorrhea is transmitted the same way as syphilis—through sexual contact. Like the spirochetes of syphilis, the bacteria of gonorrhea cannot live outside the body. They must be passed directly from mucous membrane to mucous membrane.

THE HIDER

Everything had gone right for Joanna until last week. She had graduated from college two years ago, worked a year, and then married Brad. They wanted to start a family right away, but Joanna had not been able to get pregnant. Last week the doctor told her she had chlamydia. She had never even heard of it.

The doctor said, "Joanna, doesn't it hurt when you urinate, and haven't you noticed a discharge from your vagina?"

"It doesn't hurt any more than it has for years," Joanna replied, "and I use thin pads for my light days. This disease can be treated, can't it?"

"Of course," said the doctor. "We can get you and your husband on antibiotics right away, but I can't promise that you'll be able to have a baby."

"Do I have to tell Brad? Can't you just treat me?" Joanna asked.

"If I just treat you, Brad will just reinfect you right away. Both of you have to be treated at the same time."

When Joanna told Brad, he was crushed. "I don't have any disease—I haven't noticed any pain or discharge," he said.

"The doctor said you probably wouldn't have any symptoms, but you're sure to have it if I do," Joanna replied.

"Where did you catch it anyway?" asked Brad.

"I don't know," Joanna answered. "It must have been from someone I knew before I met you."

Although chlamydia is "something old" because it has been around for centuries, it is "something new" to most people because it doesn't get a lot of publicity. It has spread so quickly that experts now estimate that about one of every 10 high school and college students have the disease, and most of them don't even know it. Its symptoms are so mild that many of those infected think they just have the flu.

Chlamydia remains unknown to many people because it is quite undramatic. It doesn't make the news. Although syphilis, gonorrhea, herpes, and AIDS all receive quite a bit of press, chlamydia does not.

Like gonorrhea and syphilis, chlamydia is transmitted through sexual contact and treated with antibiotics. It is highly contagious, so if you have sexual contact with someone who has it, you are very likely to catch it.

THE LINGERER

Fifteen-year-old Mason noticed a tingling, itching, burning feeling around his penis and scrotum. Later he noticed little sores in the area and began experiencing headaches, fever, nausea, and general aches and pains. Except for the sores on his genitals, he felt like he had the flu; but he visited the doctor anyway.

After the examination, the doctor said, "Mason, you have herpes."

Mason was stunned. "Isn't herpes incurable? Does this mean that I'll always feel this way?"

"Yes it's incurable, but you won't always feel this bad," replied the doctor. "I can give you a prescription for acyclovir that'll make you feel better, but it won't cure you. You'll always have the virus. In a few weeks it'll go into your neurons and stop bothering you as much. However, it may suddenly break out again. Some people never have another attack, but others have them three or four times a year."

"You mean that I'll feel like I have the flu several times a year for the rest of my life?" asked Mason.

"You will if your herpes acts like it does in many other people. If you're lucky, you may never have another attack," replied the doctor.

Mason left the doctor's office in shock. He still had three years of high school left. How would he ever be able to live with herpes?

Mason is not alone. Since doctors aren't required to report herpes cases, no one knows how many people really have the disease; but most doctors estimate about 20,000,000 Americans do. In addition, about another 500,000 get it each year. Since there is no cure for herpes, the total number of those afflicted grows each year.

Mason probably caught herpes like people catch the other diseases we have discussed—through sexual contact with someone who had it. However, unlike the spirochetes of syphilis or the bacteria of gonorrhea and chlamydia, the viruses causing herpes can live outside the body for some time. So it is possible, although not very likely, that he caught it by using a damp towel or another object used previously by someone who had herpes.

Unfortunately, when a woman has herpes, she faces additional risks. She is more likely to develop cancer of the cervix. In addition, if a pregnant woman has an active outbreak of herpes when her baby is about to be born, she may need a caesarian section because the baby could catch the virus during a normal birth. Babies cannot tolerate the herpes virus as well as adults. The disease can cause brain damage or even death to the newborn.

Because herpes is incurable, it made the news regularly in the early 1980s. Nearly everyone was aware of it. But now that AIDS has taken the limelight, herpes has dropped into the background. Our awareness of it is "something new," but herpes itself is "something old."

THE KILLER

We probably don't need any examples illustrating the symptoms of AIDS, Acquired Immunodeficiency Syndrome. There are no particular symptoms when people first become infected with the virus. It is a disease that destroys the body's immunity to disease. In later stages, AIDS victims simply become less and less able to fight off whatever disease they get. A simple fungus can be devastating. Cancer or pneumonia can kill much sooner than it would in a normal person.

AIDS always kills. As of January 1, 1988, more than 50,000 people had been diagnosed as having AIDS, and 28,149 had died. The number of people with AIDS is doubling every 18 months. That means 100,000 AIDS victims by the middle of 1989 and 200,000 by the beginning of 1991. No one has ever recovered from AIDS. There is no cure for it, and no vaccine to prevent it.

You probably don't know any teenagers who have died from AIDS. Teens seldom die from it because it usually takes several years from the time of infection to develop the disease. When teens are infected at 16 or 17, they are usually in their twenties before they actually come down with AIDS and die. It often takes 7–8 years to come down with the virus.

AIDS really is "something new." The first article about it appeared June 5, 1981. At first, Americans seemed to think that AIDS was a disease of male homosexuals and drug users, but that's not true. In Africa, about half the victims are women.

AIDS is usually caught like the other diseases we have discussed—through sexual contact. Unfortunately, we often hear the misleading phrase "safe sex" regarding AIDS prevention. ("Safe sex" usually refers to using a condom during intercourse.) Using a condom does not mean that a person cannot catch AIDS, only that that person is *less likely* to catch it.

AIDS is also spread directly through blood. That's how intravenous drug users catch it. That's also why doctors and dentists wear rubber gloves whenever they touch any bodily fluids. All it takes is a hangnail or chapped skin to let the virus into your body. The World Health Organization warned, "Do not share

74

items that could become contaminated with blood: for example, razors, toothbrushes, or any skin-piercing instrument" (*Reader's Digest,* June 1987).

You might ask, "If you can get AIDS from toothbrushes, can you get it from kissing?" That question is open to debate right now. You can't get AIDS from a kiss on the cheek where there is no broken skin. However, the U.S. Public Health Service suggests, "Avoid open-mouthed, intimate kissing." In 1986, the American College Health Association said, "The risk of kissing is uncertain, but deep or rough kissing increases the risk of damaging the tissues of the lips or the inside of the mouth."

The real problem with AIDS is how little we know. I have written the "facts" as they are now. Of course, as we learn more, the "facts" change. You can learn the latest information by calling the toll-free AIDS Hotline from the U.S. Public Health Service (1-800-342-AIDS). The person you talk with will not know who you are.

THE ONLY PROTECTION

If this were the late 1940s, I would probably be writing this chapter with great optimism. I would be saying that sexually transmitted diseases were nearly a thing of the past. However, to be honest, today I have to say that sexually transmitted diseases are worse than they have been for hundreds of years.

If having one of these diseases *once* gave a person immunity to the disease, perhaps we could be optimistic. Unfortunately, such is not the case. Syphilis, gonorrhea, and chlamydia can be caught again and again. Of course, once a person gets herpes or AIDS, he or she has it for life, so there's no question of reinfection.

In this chapter so far, we seem to have forgotten about our love triangle. But that's not the case. This chapter is necessary in discussing the sexual side of the triangle. God intended for us to express ourselves fully sexually only in a marriage relationship where sharing and commitment are present.

God created our world so that actions have consequences. If you cross the street against the light, you increase your chances of being hit by a car. If you smoke, you increase your chances of lung cancer. If you have sex outside marriage, you risk getting STD's. Of course, if you look carefully and cross with the light, do not smoke, and have sex only in marriage, you protect yourself from these consequences.

C. Everett Koop, former Surgeon General of the United States, has repeatedly said that the way to avoid these diseases is to "establish a mutually faithful monogamous relationship." That means you have sexual contact with only one other person who has sexual contact only with you. In other words, if you follow God's plan for expressing your sexuality in marriage with someone who is also following God's plan regarding sex, love, and dating, you have nothing to fear.

7

WHY DATE?

Two students recently attended a convention with me. As we drove to the convention, our conversation turned to dating. Martin, one of the students, stated that he'd never had a date.

Duane, the other one, immediately challenged that. "I saw you eating dinner with Sally in the cafeteria last week. Wasn't that a date?"

"No," replied Martin. "We were just eating together."

"After dinner I saw you sitting out on a bench together. Wasn't that a date?" asked Duane.

"No," replied Martin again. "We were just talking."

"OK," said Duane. "I saw you and Sally at the movie and at the grill Friday night. Surely that was a date."

"No," replied Martin once more. "We just went as friends."

"Come on, Martin," said Duane. "If those weren't dates, what in the world is a date?"

"A date is something you do when you think you might want to marry a girl. I have no interest in marrying Sally. We're just friends who have fun together."

"You don't have to be thinking about marriage to have a date," said Duane. "Just being with a girl and having fun with her is a date. Going to dinner and a movie is a date in anybody's book."

"Not in mine," said Martin. "I've never been interested in marrying anyone I've met, so I've never had a date."

The conversation went on for more than an hour. Of course, the basic disagreement was in defining the word "date." If dating means only looking for a mate, Martin has never had a date. If it means socializing with people of the opposite sex, he has had many dates.

I don't know what Sally thought about the time she'd spent with Martin, but chances are she thought she and Martin were dating. Since the invention of dating, we have confused "being friends" and "finding a mate." Let's look at how these two viewpoints were separate in Bible times.

FINDING A MATE

The courtship of Isaac and Rebekah is the most complete and typical example of finding a mate in the Bible. We find the story in Genesis 24.

Abraham, Isaac's father, was getting old and decided it was time for him to find a wife for Isaac. He called his chief servant and instructed him to "go to my country and my own relatives and get a wife for my son Isaac" (v. 4). Notice that Abraham was concerned about the cultural, religious, and family background of his future daughter-in-law.

The servant followed Abraham's instructions. "Then he prayed, 'O Lord, God of my master Abraham, give me success today' " (v. 12). He began his search by praying. He prayed for a kind, hardworking woman—one who would give him a drink and water his camels as well.

When Rebekah came along, the Bible tells us: "The girl was very beautiful, a virgin; no man had ever lain with her" (v. 16). Abraham's servant asked her for a little water. She gave him some.

"After she had given him a drink, she said, 'I'll draw water for your camels too, until they have finished drinking' " (v. 19). The servant had ten very thirsty camels, and he "watched her closely" as she carried water for them all.

Then he asked her about her family, and even asked to stay overnight. She told him about her parents. "And she added, 'We have plenty of straw and fodder, as well as room for you to spend the night' " (v. 25). She was hospitable as well as being kind, hardworking, beautiful, sexually pure, and from the right background.

"Then the man bowed down and worshiped the Lord, saying, 'Praise be to the Lord, the God of my master Abraham' " (vv. 26-27). The servant thanked God for answering his prayer. Then he met Rebekah's family and asked them about her marrying Isaac.

After Rebekah's father and brother heard a detailed description of how the servant had met Rebekah, they said, " 'This is from the Lord; we can say nothing to you one way or the other. Here is Rebekah; take her and go, and let her become the wife of your master's son, as the Lord has directed' " (vv. 50-51).

It might appear as though Rebekah had no choice in the matter, but she did. The morning after Rebekah's family had agreed to her marrying Isaac, the servant wanted to leave right away; but Rebekah's family wanted her to take 10 days to say good-bye.

"Then they said, 'Let's call the girl and ask her about it.' So they called Rebekah and asked her, 'Will you go with this man?' "

" 'I will go,' she said" (vv. 57-58).

They left right away. Rebekah took her nurse and her maids. At this point, she had not yet met Isaac or his family. She knew that Isaac had the right background and that he could support her, but she had never even seen him.

> He [Isaac] went out to the field one evening to meditate, and as he looked up, he saw camels approaching. Rebekah also looked up and saw Isaac. She got down from her camel and asked the servant, "Who is that man in the field coming to meet us?"
>
> "He is my master," the servant answered. So she took her veil and covered herself (vv. 63-65).

Although this courtship may sound strange to you, it is quite typical of the early Hebrews. "Dating" in this era had nothing to do with finding a mate. Marriage was usually arranged by the parents, with the approval of the bride and groom.

BEING FRIENDS

Since friendship had little to do with finding a mate in the Hebrew culture, people of opposite sex could be friends without others thinking anything about it. An unmarried man and woman could spend time together without other people thinking of them as a couple. This was also true in New Testament times.

Neither Jesus nor Mary, sister of Martha and Lazarus, were married. They were good friends, but no one thought of them as a couple who might marry. We read that Jesus "loved" Mary, as well as Martha and Lazarus (John 11:5). Although others criticized Mary for some things she did, there was never any hint of sexual wrong.

One time when Jesus was at the home of Mary, Martha, and Lazarus, Martha got upset with Mary, who sat at the Lord's feet listening to what He was saying. Martha was not upset that Mary was doing anything shameful, but that she was not helping with the cooking and cleaning.

Another time when Jesus was at their home, "Mary took about a pint of pure nard, an expensive perfume; she poured it on Jesus' feet and wiped His feet with her hair. And the house was filled with the fragrance of the perfume" (John 12:3).

The disciples were upset by this, but they did not suggest that Mary had done anything sexually wrong. As one of them said, "Why wasn't this perfume sold and the money given to the poor? It was worth a year's wages" (John 12:5).

Mary sat around listening to Jesus all the time, put perfume worth thousands of dollars on Him and wiped His feet with her hair. Even then, no one thought of them as anything more than good friends. It did not even occur to people of that day that there might be a romantic relationship between them.

Courtship and friendship were separate for thousands of years. But with the invention of dating, we began to mix socializing with finding a mate. No longer can single people of opposite sex just be friends without others thinking they are "more than friends."

FRIENDSHIP DATING

Since dating today means both socializing *and* finding a mate, sometimes it can lead to misunderstandings. Brady and Perry, two young college men, decided that they would experiment with a "friendship date." They asked two girls, Juanita and Sarah, to go hiking—just as friends, nothing more.

That Saturday everything seemed to go as Brady and Perry had planned. Juanita and Sarah both had fun. However, by the next week, the concept of the "friendship date" seemed to break down.

Brady and Juanita started spending more time together, and became more than just friends.

Perry thought that Sarah was beginning to like him as more than a friend. He just wanted to be friends, so for a while he tried to avoid her. Sarah wondered if she'd done something to make him mad. She hadn't. Perry and Brady had tried to separate the two parts of dating, and it just had not worked.

Since it's very difficult to separate the two parts of dating, we need to be careful about which people of the opposite sex become our best friends. As we become good friends, romantic relationships may develop.

THE KIND OF PERSON TO LOOK FOR

When talking about whom we should date, people usually quote, "Do not be yoked together with unbelievers. . . . What does a believer have in common with an unbeliever?" (2 Corinthians 6:14-15) People you date should be Christians, but that's only the first requirement. Unfortunately, some Christians make very poor husbands and wives.

The Bible has a long list of descriptions of a good spouse in the last verses of the book of Proverbs. Among the descriptions are: is of noble character; is an eager worker; helps the poor; provides for the family; has strength; has dignity; is wise; and watches over the household. How similar is this list to the one you use in looking for a date?

NOT-SO-GOOD REASONS FOR DATING

We've talked about two good reasons to date: to socialize and to find a mate. There are many other reasons—poor reasons—for dating. The poor reasons for dating fall into two categories: to get something or to get away from something.

What is there to *get* from dating? First, you might date for the prestige involved. I remember one girl in school who was considered beautiful by all the guys. Every guy who wanted to be somebody went out with her. She had more dates than anyone else in school, but graduated unmarried and without even having a boyfriend. All the guys had given their egos a boost by dating her once or twice, but none of them were interested in becoming friends with her. She had been used as a way of getting prestige.

Second, you might date to get acceptance. Everyone else is dating, and you want to be a part of them. The "in" crowd all have boyfriends and girlfriends, and to become part of them, you have to have one too. You date someone because you want a ticket to popularity, not because you want a friend or a mate.

Third, you can get revenge by dating someone. Duncan had just broken up with Jeannette. Jeanette knew that Quinn had been wanting to date her, and that Duncan could not stand Quinn. So when Quinn asked her out, she accepted immediately, thinking that she would make Duncan jealous.

Finally, you might date to get sex. Some people believe that if they spend money on dinner and a movie, their dates owe them at least petting, if not intercourse.

Now, what is there to *get away from* by dating? First, you might get away from loneliness and boredom. You may not necessarily want to be friends with the person you date, but neither do you want to be sitting home alone every weekend. It's much better to have someone around.

Second, you might date to get away from insecurity. It's comforting to know that someone will be there for you between classes, at lunch, and on weekend evenings. You may not feel at ease when you don't know what's going to happen. Dating someone means that you can settle into a routine.

Finally, you might date to get away from a bad home. If your family is always in conflict and arguing at home, it's much nicer to be at your boyfriend's or girlfriend's home where people get along.

The problem with dating to get something or to get

away from something is that you are using people. This kind of dating will work for a while, but not long. When other people realize you are using them for your own selfish reasons, they will be hurt. You can't build lasting relationships this way. Sooner or later other people will want out, unless they are using you the same way. Then you may want out of the relationship yourself.

INCREASING THE DATING SIDE

It may sound obvious, but dating—getting together with members of the opposite sex—is one of the best ways to lengthen the "dating" side of your love triangle. As you become friends with people of the opposite sex, you become more open with them. You share more and more of yourself with them.

As you spend more time with them, you will soon find that you have more to talk about than just who won the game Friday night. Your relationship will go beyond school gossip. You will begin talking about things that really matter to you.

You will begin to talk about what you want to do with your life. You will share the good things with that other person. You will laugh and have fun with each other. You will talk about things that really bother you, about your failures, and about problems at home and school. Sometimes you will cry together. Sometimes you won't even be able to talk, but you will still be able to share just by being together.

Dating is not to socialize *or* to find a mate, but to socialize *and* find a mate.

87

8

SPECTATE OR
PARTICIPATE?

True or false: The best date for a Christian couple is going to church together.

False! Going to church together is certainly an important part of a relationship, but it is not the best activity for what a "date" is to accomplish. If the purpose of dating is to lengthen the sharing (dating) side of your love triangle, going to church together is not a good date.

Typically in a worship service, a couple just sits side by side, looking ahead, listening and singing with everyone else. There is usually little chance to communicate with each other. There is little chance to talk, or even look at each other very much.

So if going to church together is not a good date, what is? Let's look at a short history of dating to get some clues.

HISTORY OF THE DATE

In *The Making of the Modern Family* (Basic Books), author Edward Shorter explains the evolution of dating over the years.

He explains that in early courtships, the whole community was involved in getting a couple together. Neighbors had "bees" at which families got together to work in the evenings. They had sewing bees, quilting bees, and husking bees. Friends had "barn-raisings" at which the men built a barn and the women cooked. Communities had festivals which everyone attended. Churches had weekly activities for families.

Young men met and courted young women with everyone from the community present. This didn't mean that they never slipped off for a moment alone; but parents, brothers, sisters, or neighbors were around most of the time when a couple were together. When it came time to marry, couples asked their parents' permission.

Gradually courtship changed so that young people could meet at youth-controlled events. These events included Sunday evening walks in which groups of young people walked through the streets singing late into the night, school dances on the weekends, and parties at the teenagers' homes.

Young men courted young women with other people of the same age present. Sometimes, as a holdover from earlier days, a chaperone representing the community was present. When it came time to marry, parents *might* be asked first, but it was no longer really expected.

In today's courtship, only the couple is present. Of course, the couple spends *some* time with parents and neighbors around, but usually as little as possible. They spend more time with other teens, but that's still not where the real courtship takes place. The couple usually come up with their own activities and carry on courtship alone.

The Bible does not tell us anything specifically about this kind of dating. However, it does tell us what our love relationships in general should be like:

> Love is patient,
> love is kind.
> It does not envy,
> it does not boast,
> it is not rude,
> it is not self-seeking,
> it is not easily angered,
> it keeps no record of wrongs.
> Love does not delight in evil
> but rejoices with the truth.
> It always protects,
> always trusts,
> always hopes,
> always perseveres.
> (1 Corinthians 13:4-7)

On most of today's dates you have the choice of watching or doing. Whether you and your date spectate or participate, think about how your relationship measures up to these four verses from 1 Corinthians 13.

SPECTATE

Probably the most common date today is the movie, a spectator date. Movies are a means of getting away from parents and other people you know. It's a way for you and your date to be alone (with a group of strangers).

Unfortunately, movies are about as good for increasing the dating side of your triangle as a morning worship service. If the movie is good, you and your date sit side by side, not talking, watching the movie. No sharing develops because no communication takes place. If you don't like the movie, you might begin to talk. But even then, you can't talk too much or the people around you will tell you to shut up.

Many school events are popular spectator dates. Ball games, though, allow more conversation opportunities than movies. At a ball game, you and your date are expected to talk with each other and with others around you. Since everyone is talking and yelling, you're not out of place. Of course, you're not likely to share anything very deep at a ball game. The dating side of your triangle may grow *a little,* but not much.

Another common spectator date is watching television or a movie on your VCR at home. This is a lot like going to the theater, with some special advantages and pitfalls. One advantage is that you and your date can usually talk while the show is on. Another advantage is that if other family members are watching with you and your date, you can get to know them as well.

One pitfall is that TV shows and scenes in a movie may come on that you don't feel good about watching. It may be embarrassing for you to have to get up and change the channel or turn it off.

Another pitfall is the possibility of watching TV alone in the house with your date. Seventy-five percent of all sex before marriage takes place at home.

With your parents working or gone for the evening, you may wind up increasing the sex side of your triangle instead of the dating side. We always made it a rule that our teens and their dates would not spend time alone in our house—or their date's house.

Although spectator dates don't do much to lengthen the dating side of your triangle, they are still good in some cases. They make excellent activities for a couple just beginning to date. They are a good way to find out if you and your date have anything in common. A spectator date allows you to find out if you can talk together at all. If not, at least you have something to hold your attention until the date is over.

Occasional spectator dates are good all the time you are dating—even after you are married. The problem comes when your whole relationship is built on spectator dates. They do not give you the chance to really be a part of the important things in another person's life.

PARTICIPATE

The number of things you can do on a date to get to know another person is practically unlimited. Many books have been written about creative dating. Let's look at a number of possible participation dates. Use the ideas that interest you. Then come up with some creative ones of your own.

● *Team Sports*

You and your date can get a group together to play volleyball, flag football, basketball, softball, soccer, etc. You could do this in your neighborhood or with your church group.

● *"Backyard" Sports*

You might want to play some sports in which fewer

people are involved—or even just the two of you. These could include croquet, badminton, lawn darts, horseshoes, and tetherball. Or, if you prefer, you could simply throw a Frisbee around. Ping-Pong or darts can be fun when the weather is bad outside.

Other sports, such as miniature golf, tennis, or bowling require special equipment not found in your "backyard," but most communities have them at a reasonable price. When playing these sports with your date, you'll find out how well you get along together in losing, as well as winning.

● *Outdoor Sports*

Outdoor sports are different in various parts of the country. If you live near water, you have many options available. You can take your date fishing. If the fish aren't biting, you can water ski. You can go canoeing or sailboating together. You can go swimming, or just lay on a beach together.

Some people like shooting. You can go hunting with your date. If you don't like killing animals, shoot them with a camera. If you like shooting a gun, but not killing animals, shoot at cans or targets. BBs and .22 caliber rifle shells cost little for an afternoon of shooting.

During the winter you and your date can go sledding together if you live near hills. You can go skiing, either downhill or cross-country. When the snow will pack, you can build snowmen or have a snowball fight.

No matter where you live you can go for a walk together. You might even want to go on an extended hike, taking a day pack with food for the day. You can bicycle together anywhere you have a decent road or path. Horseback riding is another fun participation date. Flying a kite together can be fun. If you and your date both like to jog, you can make that a regular date several times a week.

● *Table Games*

Maybe you prefer indoor games. These games can provide a lot of conversation if you play ones that don't require much thought or don't last too long after people start to lose. Chess is great, but not for developing sharing, because the players are busy thinking about their next moves. Monopoly is fun, but when people start dropping out, they may be out of the game for an hour or more.

Games such as Pit, Uno, Trivial Pursuit, and Pictionary are fast-moving, and keep everyone involved.

Walking through the game section of a toy store will give you many more ideas. Since many games cost around $25, try to find someone who has a game and play it once before you buy it. While in the toy store, stop by the puzzle section. If you and your date both like puzzles, putting one together can be a good way to increase the dating side of your triangle.

● *Places of Interest*

You can find places of interest nearly anywhere. You and your date can visit state parks, national parks, museums, battlefields, and old forts. If you don't know where these are, call your local chamber of commerce, or look in your paper. Also, don't overlook visits to an everyday place such as a farm, an airport, and even a cemetery.

● *Special Events*

Most communities have special events during the year that make great dates. During the summer, many counties have fairs. Shopping malls have special events from time to time. Holidays often mean parades or plays. Often church youth groups sponsor retreats and fund-raisers. Most of these events would serve as ideal participation dates. You can find out about special events through your local paper and the bulletin at church.

● *Volunteer Work*

Instead of looking for entertainment, try serving someone else. Visit a nursing home or children's home with your date. Volunteer to be substitute teachers for children's Sunday School classes or assist a teacher in Vacation Bible School. Rake lawns, mow grass, paint houses, or wash windows together for some older person in the community. A call to your church office, senior citizen's center, or community service agency will provide you with many opportunities.

● *Food-Related Activities*

Food preparation, eating, and cleanup can make good dates. Unfortunately, most people think the only food-related thing you can do on a date is eat. Cooking can be just as fun. Have a picnic in which you make the sandwiches together. Have a cookout. Do the dishes together.

If you don't know what to cook, buy a cookbook and find something neither of you has eaten before. Walk down the aisles of a large supermarket and buy something you have never heard of. Cook it together, eat, and clean up.

● *Everyday Tasks*

Most teens don't think of everyday tasks as dates, but they're what you will wind up doing together most—if you marry the person you are dating. So why not "practice" ahead of time? Wash the car together. Make Christmas gifts together. Go shopping (at least window-shopping) together.

Get out family albums and get acquainted with each other's families. Work on hobbies together. Go to a flea market or farmer's market and buy something. Weed the garden together, refinish a piece of furniture, or paint something. The possibilities are endless. And these are just the kinds of things you may wind up doing together in the future.

RATING YOURSELF

Earlier in this chapter, we looked at the general characteristics of love in relationships in 1 Corinthians 13. Now let's put these characteristics to practical use. Using a scale of 1–10, rate yourself and the person you're dating on each characteristic on the list below.

	Me	My Date
Love is patient,	_____	_____
love is kind.	_____	_____
It does not envy,	_____	_____
it does not boast,	_____	_____
it is not rude,	_____	_____
it is not self-seeking,	_____	_____
it is not easily angered,	_____	_____
it keeps no record of wrongs.	_____	_____
Love does not delight in evil	_____	_____
but rejoices with the truth.	_____	_____
It always protects,	_____	_____
always trusts,	_____	_____

always hopes,   ⸻   ⸻
always perseveres.   ⸻   ⸻
(1 Corinthians 13:4-7)

How did you and your date measure up to ideal love? What areas do you need to work on?

MEETING FRIENDS AND FAMILY

As you become more serious about dating one person, you and your date should spend time with other people your own age. In the future, you and your spouse will have to get along with others, so it's important to see how you interact with others as a couple. You will also find it helpful to see how your date gets along with the whole community. Can you both be comfortable with people of all ages? If not, what will you do in the future?

Most important is finding out how you get along with each other's parents. You should spend time as a couple with each other's families, both in everyday things and in special events. You do not marry just one person, but a whole family. Your spouse will bring the way his or her family does things to your marriage, and if you can't get along with the family now, you will have trouble getting along with your spouse later.

As you date you should both spectate and participate. When your dating gets more serious, you should do less spectating and more participating. As you do this, the dating side of your love triangle will lengthen.

9

THE DATELESS

Marissa was sitting in her room listening to her stereo. It was Friday night, and she would have much rather been at the ball game, but no one had asked her. This was not the only time she had spent a Friday night at home alone. As a matter of fact, she had only been to one game all year. It seemed like no one ever asked her out. She wondered what was wrong with her.

That same evening, Phil was watching a movie on TV with his little brother and sister. He too would rather have been at the game, but he didn't want to go alone. Twice that week he had started to ask Marissa for a date to the game, but just wasn't able to do it. He wondered what was wrong with him.

Marissa and Phil are not the only people sitting at home alone on weekends. A recent study found that one out of every three high school students almost never dates. You may be like Phil and Marissa, and think that you are the only teenager alive without a date. You may be wondering what's wrong with you.

WHY AREN'T YOU DATING?

In many cases teens who aren't dating know exactly why they aren't dating, but can do nothing about it. They may not be allowed to date because their parents believe they are too young. They may not have a car or enough money to date. (Of course, they don't really *need* a car or money to date, but some people are convinced they do.) Maybe the only person they care about dating is already dating someone else. This chapter is not for these people.

Some teens who aren't dating just don't care to date. They may not know anyone they want to date. They may enjoy being with a group, but not feel at ease when they are alone with just one other person. *They* may believe that they are too young, just not ready to date yet. This chapter is not for these people either.

This chapter is for people who don't date (or who don't date much) but would like to.

If we look at why people *are* asked for dates, we may get a clue about why certain others *are not* asked. One major reason why people ask someone out for a first date is physical attractiveness. Although it should not be so, study after study has shown that attractive teens have more dates with different people than those who are less attractive.

Let me tell you about Bertha. When I rode the bus to high school, Bertha got on near the end of the route, and no one wanted her to sit with him. Bertha was the first one we could see as we approached her bus stop because she was about 30 pounds overweight. Of course, she soon became "Big Bertha" to us. Her clothes looked like she had slept in them (and that was long before it was fashionable to look like that).

Her hair was almost indescribable. It looked like her mom or dad had cut it, like it hadn't been combed in a week, and like it hadn't been washed in a month. Everyday Bertha came down the aisle of the bus, hunched over, kind of shuffling along. If she sat next to me or across the aisle, my nose soon told me that she hadn't had a bath in a week or two, and that her family liked onions and garlic.

Now I usually don't recommend TV to teenagers, but Bertha could have benefited from watching some commercials. Advertisers warn us about what people in our culture find unattractive, and then try to get us to use their products to make ourselves more attractive.

Manufacturers of toothpaste and mouthwash would have told Bertha about her breath problem. Manufacturers of soaps, deodorants, perfumes, and colognes would have told Bertha about her body odors. Manufacturers of detergent would have told her to wash her clothes more often.

Manufacturers of shampoos, permanents, conditioners, hair dryers, and curling irons would have warned Bertha about the condition of her hair. Manufacturers of clothes would have told her what styles would look good on her. Weight Watchers would have warned her about her weight.

Bertha should have listened to what teachers said in health class about posture because most people find that a person who is slumped over, and who shuffles along with a frown on his or her face is less attractive than someone standing straight, walking confidently, and smiling. Bertha needed a friend or teacher to tell her about this part of her appearance.

All these aspects of physical appearance influence whether or not you get a first date. (I don't think Bertha ever got that first date in high school.) Concentrating on your physical appearance will not automatically get you a date, but it will increase your chances.

But to keep a relationship going, you have to do more than just *look* good. Celeste had everything Bertha lacked. She was attractive and had more first dates than any other girl in my class. Her problem was that she thought the world revolved around herself and her friends. After two or three dates the guys got tired of hearing "And then she said . . . and then Joanie said . . . and then . . ."

Celeste also seemed to be critical of everyone not in her group. She was smart and she knew it. The problem was that she used her intelligence to make cutting remarks about others. She was fun to be with for a while, but people quickly got tired of her.

Some people don't date because they are afraid to *ask*. Jeff was so shy that he could hardly talk to a girl, much less ask her for a date. He was 17 and had never had a date.

Still other people don't date for biblical reasons. Melinda turned down three dates in one month. Adrian wanted to date her, but Melinda took "Do not be yoked together with unbelievers" (2 Corinthians 6:14) seriously. Adrian didn't go to church, and Melinda decided that since one of the purposes of dating was to find a mate, she would not date Adrian (or anyone else who was not a Christian).

It's not possible to list *all* the reasons a person may not date. We've looked at some of the most common reasons, but there are many more. The problem with many reasons for not dating is that often you don't recognize them yourself. The best way to find out is to ask some older trusted friend, such as a teacher or pastor. You can't tell when your breath is bad or how other people view you. What you need is someone who will be helpfully honest with you.

Of course, the other possibility is that you are fine and the other teens you know are all wanting to date for wrong reasons. They may be looking for prestige, acceptance, revenge, or sex. They may be trying to get away from boredom, insecurity, or bad homes. You're better off not dating these people. Your helpfully honest friend will tell you whether the problem lies with you or with others.

THE "L" WORD: LONELINESS

The loneliness that comes from not dating is *not* a result of the invention of adolescence. It is the result of creation. Men and women were created with a need for each other. We were all created with a need for the sharing we can have only with another human being.

God created Adam and placed him in the Garden of Eden. Adam was to take care of the Garden. Even before the Fall, the Lord said, "It is not good for the man to be alone. I will make a helper suitable for him"

(Genesis 2:18). Obviously the plants in the Garden had not solved Adam's loneliness.

God brought all the animals and birds to Adam. "So the man gave names to all the livestock, the birds of the air and all the beasts of the field. But for Adam no suitable helper was found" (Genesis 2:20). Like the plants, the animals did not solve Adam's loneliness.

Finally, God created woman and brought her to Adam. "The man said, 'This is now bone of my bones and flesh of my flesh; she shall be called "woman," for she was taken out of man'" (Genesis 2:23). Adam immediately recognized that this person was like himself, and that she would solve his loneliness problem.

Ever since Creation, people have struggled with loneliness. In the Old Testament, David said, "My friends and companions avoid me because of my wounds; my neighbors stay far away" (Psalm 38:11). In the New Testament, Paul said, "At my first defense, no one came to my support, but everyone deserted me. May it not be held against them" (2 Timothy 4:16).

Most of us identify with Charlie Brown in the "Peanuts" comic strip when he is the only one in the class not to get a valentine. We sympathize with Ziggy when he is alone because even his psychiatrist will not listen to him.

Having people around does not mean you will not be lonely. The most lonely time in my life was when I was a student at Wayne State University in Detroit. My family was 300 miles north and my future wife was 400 miles south. I was in the middle of 4.5 million people, but knew only two of them. I was alone in a crowd.

Lonely people usually report feeling empty. They say they feel like something is missing inside. They feel like they are hollow, just "shells" going through the motions of living.

They report feelings of depression. They feel sad, which makes them less fun to be with, and more likely to be rejected by others—which makes them lonelier. People who are down in the dumps all the time are not fun to be with.

Lonely people, like Marissa and Phil at the beginning of this chapter, often wonder what's wrong with them. They have low self-esteem. They feel unwanted, unpopular, and angry or guilty.

All of these negative feelings come with loneliness, and most of us have experienced them at some time in our lives. Teenagers who are not dating often feel them. They don't just need *people* around, they need to be in the *right relationship* with the people around them. In the Old Testament, Job did not need three "friends" to condemn him and a wife to tell him to "curse God and die." As he put it, "Oh, that I had someone to hear me!" (Job 31:35)

DO SOMETHING ABOUT IT

Since we were created for sharing, we must find a sharing relationship with someone. If the reason you aren't dating is something that can be changed, change it and begin to share with someone through dating. If it's something you can't change, find sharing in other ways.

You may develop a sharing relationship with someone of the same sex. The most famous example of this is David and Jonathan (King Saul's son) in the Old

Testament. After David had become a hero by killing Goliath, "Jonathan became one in spirit with David, and he loved him as himself" (1 Samuel 18:1).

Remember that Samuel had anointed David to become the next king, to take Prince Jonathan's place. Even knowing that, Jonathan became David's closest friend. They could talk with each other about anything, even the fact that Jonathan's father was trying to kill David. After Jonathan gave David a final warning to run for his life, the two wept together. "Jonathan said to David, 'Go in peace, for we have sworn friendship with each other in the name of the Lord' " (1 Samuel 20:42).

You can make several close friends and find sharing and friendship with them. When our son, Keith, was in high school, he and several of his friends started "FFF"—the Fellowship of the Fabulous Four. (The next year it grew to five, but was still "FFF.") These guys met every Wednesday for supper. They ate, talked, and prayed together. They shared their hopes, dreams, and difficult times.

You may find sharing and friendship in your church youth group. Our youth group had about 10 people in one grade, and although they seldom dated each other, everyone in that grade became very close. They had parties together, sharing their lives with each other. I still remember their final party in our backyard after graduation. They just sat around and talked about their years of high school together.

Although it is less likely if you go to a public high school, you may find sharing on a team or in a club. Athletic teams are known for their team spirit, but you can find it on speech teams and academic teams as well. Our son, Kent, helped begin a prayer group of students from all churches in both towns that go to our county high school. They met for 10 minutes each morning for prayer and sharing.

Of course, your best friend is God. Jesus, knowing that His disciples would eventually desert Him, said, "You will leave Me all alone. Yet I am not alone, for My Father is with Me" (John 16:32). Jesus also said, "And I will ask the Father, and He will give you another Counselor to be with you forever" (John 14:16). The Holy Spirit will never leave you.

Your most important relationship is with God. If sin stands between you and God, you may feel lonely even with many friends. Keep your relationship with God an open, sharing one—whether you are dating or not.

THE SHARING RISK

You need friendship and sharing, and if you are not finding it in dating, you can find it in other ways. The hardest problem is to get people to share, to get beyond things that don't really matter to them. This is true in dating and marriage as well as in friendship.

When you find a group or an individual with whom you want to begin a sharing relationship, start to share yourself. If the other person or persons also want a sharing relationship, they will begin to share as well. Of course, if they don't want that kind of relationship, they won't share, so you take the risk of feeling foolish.

You also take another risk. The people you share with may not keep what you tell them in confidence. You may tell them something you don't want anyone else to know, and find out later that they spread it around. This means that as you start to share, you should not share the deepest thoughts and feelings you have. Sharing is based on trust. As time goes on and friendship increases, you will be able to share more and more.

Whether you find friendship through dating or in other ways, *do not* give up until you find it. You *need* a sharing relationship with at least one other person.

10

READY FOR A COMMITMENT?

So far we've talked about sex and dating, but they are only two sides of your love triangle. Without the commitment of *love,* your triangle is incomplete, lacking a major part.

A good example of an incomplete relationship is found in the Old Testament story of Samson. "One day Samson went to Gaza, where he saw a prostitute. He went in to spend the night with her" (Judges 16:1). It's obvious that Samson liked sex.

"Some time later, he fell in love with a woman in the Valley of Sorek whose name was Delilah" (Judges 16:4). Since Samson frequently slept at Delilah's house, we can assume that the sex side of the triangle in their relationship was quite large.

Now, if you know anything about Samson, you probably know of his great strength. Quite possibly, Samson was the strongest person who ever lived. The source of Samson's great strength was a secret known only to him and his parents. However, Delilah wanted to know. When she asked him to tell her his secret, he didn't want to, so he made up an answer. The dating side of his triangle was not very long yet. He was not ready to share with her.

Of course, Delilah was upset when she found out that Samson had not told her the truth. She asked him again, and he made up another lie. The dating side of his triangle was still short.

Delilah was even angrier. Samson had lied to her again, and she felt like a fool. A third time she asked him. And a third time Samson made up a lie. He was not sharing himself and his special secret with her, and she knew it.

Then she said to him, "How can you say, 'I love you,' when you won't confide in me? This is the third time you have made a fool of me and haven't told me the secret of your great strength." With such nagging she prodded him day after day until he was tired to death.

So he told her everything. "No razor has ever been used on my head," he said, "because I have been a Nazirite set apart to God since birth. If my head were shaved, my strength would leave me, and I would become as weak as any other man" (Judges 16:15-17).

Delilah finally got him to confide in her. The fourth time she asked, Samson told her everything. He talked with her at a deeper level than he had ever talked with anyone other than his parents. In doing so, he lengthened the dating side of his triangle.

Although both the sex and dating sides of Samson's triangle were large, the love side was still short. He and Delilah had little commitment to each other and, as a result, Samson became a prisoner of the Philistines, had his eyes gouged out, and finally died with the Philistines.

Perhaps the *consequences* of your having an unbalanced love triangle won't be quite as dramatic as Samson's, but developing the love side of your triangle is every bit as vital to you as it was to Samson. In our society, we've developed a series of stages in relationships in which the love side of our triangle gradually grows. These stages could be labeled: admiration, dating, and commitment.

ADMIRATION

You can't begin to commit yourself to someone you don't notice. So obviously the first step in a relationship is to notice the other person and begin to admire him or her. Usually this initial noticing depends on physical appearance.

Sometimes the noticing occurs the first time you meet. I can still remember the first time I saw my wife. She was standing on the steps in the Danville Jail on a Sunday morning in September. (We were there to hold services, not to serve time.) As I walked back to campus, I said to my roommate, "I'm going to date that girl."

Sometimes the noticing is really "seeing" for the first time a person you have known all your life. Maybe you had always thought of him or her as the skinny

115

kid who caused you trouble. Then suddenly you notice that he or she is an attractive person.

When this happens, you decide to "notice" him or her again—you begin to *admire* the person. Don noticed Paula at chorus rehearsal. He followed her to find where her locker was. Then day after day he would walk down that hall, even though he had no classes there, hoping to catch a glimpse of her at her locker.

You've probably done something like this. You find out where the other person lives, then find excuses to go down that street. If you know that the person sits about half way down on the right side in church, you sit about three seats further back. Then your heart beats faster when he or she sits right where you expected.

At this point, the love side of your triangle has just started to grow. You have made a decision to do something about being near a person. You may never even have spoken to that person, but you're thinking about him or her.

DATING

Admiration can go on for a long time, then end without the other person ever knowing he or she was being admired. Of course, in other cases it can lead to *dating*.

I had told my roommate that I was going to date the girl I saw on the steps of the jail. So that week when I saw her going into the library, I asked her for a date. She said yes. Then she found someone who knew me and asked her my name. Obviously, she hadn't noticed and admired me!

At this point—the first date—the love side of your triangle increases its growth rate, because you have not just made a decision to be in another person's presence, you've made a commitment to spend an evening together. As we mentioned earlier, the first date is usually a spectator date, one where you can talk to each other, but where periods of silence are not embarrassing.

When the date is over, so is the commitment. The two of you may know each other a little better, but you don't have to go on with the relationship if you don't want to. Either (or both) of you can decide that this love will not grow.

Of course, it's best when both people come to the same decision. If one wants to continue, but the other doesn't, you can have some awkward times. However, when you say, "Good-night" after that first date you should both realize that it may be the end of the relationship. This is usually true for the first few dates you have with a person, especially if you both date others in between.

Each time you date that person, you increase the love side of your triangle a little. That person comes to expect more and more that you will date him or her again, and again, and again.

COMMITMENT

While there is always a marked difference between admiring and dating, that difference is not always present as you change from dating to *commitment*. The more you date a person, the less conscious you become of what the person *looks* like, and more conscious of what the person *is* like. Appearance becomes

117

less important and personality more important.

Sometimes two people consciously decide to make a commitment or "go together." This usually means they will date only each other—until further notice. In your parents' day this was called "going steady," and the couple often wore each other's class rings. Then, "going together" was a real increase in the commitment they made to each other.

Today, this commitment is not always so formal, but the increase in the love side of the triangle is usually just as great. When two people begin to date more and more, they sometimes come to the understanding that they are "going together" without even talking about it. Soon they expect to date only each other until one of them tells the other that it's time to break up.

Before "going together," you and the person you're dating should ask yourselves two questions. The first one is *"When* should we begin going together?" Many teenagers start going together before they are old enough to handle it. This is too much commitment while you are in junior high, and perhaps even early in high school. It should begin in late high school or college.

The question of "when" is best answered when we look at the second question, *"Why* should we go together?" There are advantages to going together— and disadvantages. Let's begin with the advantages.

We all like to feel secure, and going with someone gives us the feeling of security. You don't have to worry about whether you'll have a date Friday night. You can relax during the week and not worry about asking or being asked.

A second advantage is that your self-esteem will grow. You'll be able to relax and "be yourself" with the other person. It's easier to feel good about ourselves when someone likes us just the way we are. Since you don't have the pressure of trying to impress your date, you can have a good time, enjoy yourself, and know that you'll be liked.

A third advantage of a "going-together commitment" is that you can develop a deeper friendship with the other person. The dating side of your triangle will grow. If you're going together, you'll be able to have more participation dates. You can hardly ask someone to come over and wash the car with you for a first date. But if you're going together, you can have a great time washing the car.

The advantages of going together sound great, but now let's look at the disadvantages. When you go together and make a commitment to date only each other, you limit friendships with other people of the opposite sex. You'll miss getting to know many people. There is also a tendency to become possessive, and feelings of jealousy come up when you see the other person with someone else.

A second disadvantage is that when you go with someone, you open yourself to be hurt. The more you share of yourself with someone else, the more you can be hurt. The hurt may come from something as mild as feeling like the other person is taking you for granted; or it may be as much as having the other person tell his or her friends something you meant to keep just between the two of you. Before you go with someone, make sure you can take the hurts that may come with it.

A third disadvantage is that when people go together, the sex sides of their triangles also tend to grow. As they make more commitment to each other and share more, they are likely to want to express their love physically. They begin to ask, "What's next?" After going together, the next step is usually engagement, followed by marriage, as the love side of the triangle grows. However, if you are young, engagement and marriage are a long way off. So you may begin to get too physical for the commitment you make to each other.

LOVE

The love side of the triangle is best defined as the agape love of the New Testament. The sex side of your triangle refers to your motivations. The dating side refers to your emotions. The love side of your triangle refers to your cognitions (thinking) and volitions (will). Agape love is rational. In it, you make decisions about commitments.

This is the kind of love that can be commanded. Jesus said, "As the Father has loved Me, so have I loved you. Now remain in My love. . . . My command is this: Love each other as I have loved you" (John 15:9, 12). Since this is not referring to our feelings, we can *decide* whether or not we want to love a person with this kind of love.

John wrote that we are to love this way. "This is the message you heard from the beginning: We should love one another" (1 John 3:11). "I am not writing you a new command but one we have had from the beginning. I ask that we love one another" (2 John 5). We *make up our mind* to love someone.

Sometimes people think that agape love is always good, but that's not so. Jesus said, "Woe to you Pharisees, because you love [agape] the most important seats in the synagogues and greetings in the marketplaces" (Luke 11:43). John said, "This is the verdict: Light has come into the world, but men loved [agape] darkness instead of light because their deeds were evil" (John 3:19).

Paul said, "For Demas, because he loved [agape] this world, has deserted me and has gone to Thessalonica" (2 Timothy 4:10). Obviously people who are not Christians have agape love. Jesus said, "If you love [agape] those who love [agape] you, what credit is that to you? Even 'sinners' love [agape] those who love [agape] them" (Luke 6:32). Agape love is not something you *feel*; it is something you *decide* to *do*.

God commanded this same kind of love in the Old Testament. In Deuteronomy 5, Moses repeated the Ten Commandments. Then he summarized them with a command: "Love the Lord your God with all your heart and with all your soul and with all your strength" (Deuteronomy 6:5).

In the preceding chapter we looked at the friendship between David and Jonathan. They had agape love for each other. They decided they would make commitments to one another. "Jonathan made a covenant with David because he loved him as himself" (1 Samuel 18:3). Agape love makes commitments to others. This may seem calculated and intellectual, but that is exactly what the love side of your triangle is.

This kind of love does not develop instantly, but begins to grow as you spend time with another person. As you date, the love side of your triangle will gradually grow. You won't "make covenants" or "reaffirm oaths" after a date or two, but as this side of your triangle grows, you will find yourself making commitments to that other person.

GROWTH OF THE LOVE SIDE

As the love side of your triangle grows, so can the other two. Your love triangle can become more and more what Jesus talked about when He was asked about the most important commandment.

"Love the Lord your God with all your heart and with all your soul and with all your mind and with all your strength." The second is this: "Love your neighbor as yourself." There is no commandment greater than these (Mark 12:30-31).

Jesus quoted Moses' summary of the Ten Commandments, and this summary included all the aspects of love in our love triangle. The heart, as used here, refers to our emotions, the dating side of our triangle. The mind refers to our thinking, the love side of our triangle. The strength refers to our body, the sex side of our triangle.

Notice that both Moses and Jesus tell us to love with our soul. This means that we are to love the other person with our whole being. When God created man, He breathed the breath of life into him and man became a living soul, or a "living being" (Genesis 2:7). When we love someone, God or another person, we are to love them with all of our being.

As was mentioned in earlier chapters, we must be very careful to whom we make commitments. We began this chapter looking at the relationship of Samson and Delilah. Delilah had none of the characteristics of Rebekah mentioned in chapter 7. She had none of the characteristics of love mentioned in chapter 8 (1 Corinthians 13). She was a prime example of the warning in Proverbs 31:30, "Charm is deceptive, and beauty is fleeting."

As the love side of your triangle grows when you decide to make a commitment to someone, you may have to face the problem of making the side smaller. What happens when a couple decides to *decrease* their love? Breaking love commitments is the subject of our next chapter.

11

BREAKING UP

One summer, I was helping build a house to pay my college expenses. At lunchtime several of us working on the house took a ride past my house. I had a letter from my girlfriend waiting for me. Sitting in the backseat, I opened it and read it—amid many comments from the other guys on the job.

In an earlier chapter I told you about meeting Bonnie at a jail one Sunday morning. We had eight or nine dates that first year. The next year we had dated steadily. But during this particular summer we were 500 miles apart.

That afternoon I hung drywall. A couple hours later when the electrician went back to finish wiring outlets in the room where I was working, he discovered that I had covered most of the outlets. I was supposed to cut holes through the drywall for the outlets, but I forgot. This led to many more comments about my lunchtime letter.

What they did not know, and I did not tell them, was that it was a "Dear John" letter. I had been dumped and I was in pain. It hurt too much to talk with anyone about it right then.

Many of you probably have already experienced a breakup in a relationship, and the rest of you probably will. In fact, if you date someone regularly without marrying, you *have* to either break up or date that person for the rest of your life.

Even if you get engaged to the person you're dating, there is a 50 percent chance that you'll break your engagement. The half of you who *do* end up getting married face a 50 percent chance that your marriage will eventually end in divorce. The point is, nearly everyone goes through a break-up at some time in his or her life.

Breaking up hurts. Two psychologists developed a scale to measure stress in terms of life's changes. They called it the Social Readjustment Rating Scale, and asked people to rate events in their lives in terms of how much readjustment would be needed. The event causing the most stress was death of a spouse; the second was divorce; and third was marital separation. These were the three worst events people could think of.

Of course, we're not talking about breaking up a marriage relationship in this chapter. But breaking up after dating someone for a while brings the same kind of hurt and stress, just less of it. Anytime you part and break up a love triangle, it hurts—and the larger the triangle, the more it hurts.

WHY BREAK UP?

There are many different reasons for breaking up, some good and some bad. For instance, you may break up because you and the person you're dating find yourselves in constant conflict. It may seem like you spend most of your time together either arguing or making up. As you've shared more about yourselves in the relationship, you've not liked what you found out about each other.

You may break up because you find that the two of you have different goals in life. For example, you may dream about being a Bible translator living in a primitive jungle while the person you're dating dreams of owning a chain of fast-food restaurants in large cities. Both of you may be Christians, but you have different goals.

You may break up because you discover that you're not ready for the commitment you've made. You may still want to be friends with *many* people, not tied to just one.

You may break up because you find that the two of you have increased the sex side of your triangle too much. One of you may want to decrease it, but the other doesn't.

You may break up because the person you're dating abuses you. He or she may do this physically or verbally. She may call it a "love tap," but it hurts, and she does it over and over. He may ridicule you and make you feel stupid. Remember—this kind of behavior always gets worse, not better, after marriage.

Sometimes you can't put your finger on why you want to break up. You just know that the two of you are not meant for each other.

WHY NOT TO BREAK UP

Now let's look at some reasons you shouldn't break up. You shouldn't break up just because you're angry with the other person and want to get even. Even if he or she has hurt you, revenge is not a good reason to break up.

A disagreement or two is not a good reason for breaking up. You'll disagree with *everyone* about *something,* no matter who you date. You must learn how to work out those disagreements agreeably. Of course, if you can't work out the disagreements, or if you find out that you have constant disagreements, you should break up.

Finally, breaking up because you're "tired" of the other person is not a good reason. We all have to work to keep our relationships fresh. You've heard that "variety is the spice of life." That doesn't mean a variety of *triangles* with *different* people. It means keeping variety in *one love triangle.*

HOW TO BREAK UP

Once you've decided that you should break up, how do you do it? Again, there are right and wrong ways to approach it. Since the Bible does not talk specifically about dating, it makes no mention of breaking up. However, the last part of Ephesians 4 gives us some good principles to follow which can be applied to the process of breaking up.

> Therefore each of you must put off falsehood and speak truthfully to his neighbor. . . . Do not let any unwholesome talk come out of your mouths, but only what is helpful for building others up

128

according to their needs, that it may benefit those who listen. . . . Get rid of all bitterness, rage and anger, brawling and slander, along with every form of malice. Be kind and compassionate to one another, forgiving each other, just as in Christ God forgave you (Ephesians 4:25, 29, 31-32).

As I see it, the principles of parting, or breaking up, can be summarized in eight "P" words. Parting should be done promptly, preparedly, prayerfully, personally, privately, politely, with probity, and permanently.

Part *promptly*. When you've made the decision to break up, do it soon. Don't try to keep a dying relationship alive. You can keep pretending that everything is all right, but both of you will be miserable, perhaps for weeks or months.

Part *preparedly*. Give some thought about what you're going to say before you talk to the other person. If you prepare, you may prevent additional pain. Remember that breaking up is likely to hurt, so think about what to say.

Part *prayerfully*. Prayer is part of your preparation. Pray for the other person, and pray for yourself as you break up. However, do not use "God led me" as a reason for breaking up. In most cases, that's just a cop-out.

Part *personally*. Don't write a letter or make a phone call if you can actually go see the person. Of course, if you and the person you're dating are far apart, the breaking up must be done by less personal methods; but usually it's possible to talk directly to him or her.

Part *privately*. Breaking up during lunch at school with others at the table isn't a good idea. A better idea would be to take a walk together through a park where you can talk alone.

Part *politely*. In the Ephesians 4 passage, Paul urges us to say helpful things, to build other people up, to be kind, and to be compassionate. In your preparation, think of the nicest way to say what you must say.

Part with *probity*. (No, I don't use that word all the time, but it begins with "P.") "Probity" means honesty or truth. You need to be honest with the other person. Don't say nasty things, but don't say overly nice things if you don't mean them.

Part *permanently*. This doesn't mean that the two of you can never get together again, but that the break should be complete *for now*. The other person may promise to change, threaten to do something terrible, or break into tears—but if you've decided to break up, do it. Don't change your mind during the breaking up.

The wrong ways to part usually involve saying too little or too much. You can say so little that the other person doesn't know what's wrong. I remember how poorly I broke up with the first girl I dated steadily. I simply started avoiding her, and after a while she came to me in tears, wondering what was wrong.

On the other hand, saying too much can be just as bad. You don't want to say everything you're thinking. Don't hurt the other person with angry, slanderous, unwholesome words, but speak the truth in love.

RELIEVED?

Teresa was glad it was over. She'd been thinking about breaking up with Duane for two weeks. At first,

130

she didn't know whether to break up or not. She finally decided it had to be done, and she did it. It had gone well. She and Duane were still friends. Things were awkward when they met in the hall at school, but they said, "Hi."

Duane was glad it was over too. Things hadn't been going well between him and Teresa for a couple months. He had just about decided to break up with her when she broke up with him. He didn't really want to date anyone else, but at least he didn't feel tied to Teresa.

This is the best outcome of a breakup. Duane and Teresa's relationship was dying. One of them broke it off, and both of them were glad. They still felt awkward around each other, and they probably will for some time, but they can still be friends.

HURTING?

It would be nice if all breakups came out like Duane and Teresa's. Unfortunately, that's not the case. Usually the one doing the breaking up is relieved, and the other is hurting.

When someone has just broken up with you and you are suddenly "not dating" again, you feel even lonelier than you did before you started going together. You have that empty feeling because the other person isn't there with you.

You again begin to wonder what is wrong with you. You thought everything was going fine, and suddenly the other person doesn't want to be with you anymore. You feel confused. You don't feel like doing anything but sitting at home and watching television.

More than that, you have to think about starting to

date again. What if no one wants to date you? Can you ever trust anyone again? After all, you shared some of your deepest secrets with that other person, and now he or she doesn't want to be with you anymore.

The feelings a person experiences in the breakup of a relationship are similar to the feelings a person experiences in the death of a loved one. Dr. Elizabeth Kubler-Ross found that people go through five stages in dealing with death. You will find these same five stages in the death of a romantic relationship.

The first stage is *denial*. You can't believe it. You thought everything was fine between the two of you, and suddenly it's over. You think there must be some mistake—surely the other person misunderstood something you did. You hope that it's all a bad dream, and that tomorrow it won't be true.

The second stage is *anger*. When you finally believe it, you get angry. You feel like shouting or throwing things. You feel like hurting the other person, perhaps telling some of the things he or she has shared with you.

The third stage is *bargaining*. When anger does no good, you try to strike some sort of deal to keep the relationship alive. You might make a promise to change if you can just keep going together. You might threaten to do something harmful if you break up.

The fourth stage is *depression*. When the bargaining doesn't work, you become sad. You don't feel like doing anything except sitting around, feeling sorry for yourself.

The fifth and final stage is *acceptance*. You finally accept the fact that the relationship is over and begin to rebuild your life. This whole process takes time and you feel grief while it is happening, but it passes.

Paul's words in Philippians 3:13-14 apply here: "Forgetting what is behind and straining toward what is ahead, I press on toward the goal to win the prize for which God has called me heavenward in Christ Jesus." This passage gives us the two important pieces of advice for when we start over after a break-up.

First, it's important that we not try to recapture the past. The relationship is over. Although you still want to be friends with that other person, don't try to see him or her too much. You may be able to get together again, but for a while you need to be apart.

Some people try to recapture the past with a new person. Getting into a new love relationship too soon isn't a good idea. All you're doing is substituting that new person for the old one, and you need time to get over the old one. Rebound romances rarely last, and soon you'll be going through the pain of breaking up again.

Second, it's important that we press on toward the goal. This is your chance to renew and deepen relationships with God and other people. God can, through this experience, help you grow. There will be an empty spot in your life, but you can fill it with new friendships. We will all experience a breakup, and we can all grow through it.

12

TYING THE KNOT

Some of you may be more effective for God if you stay single. As the Apostle Paul put it:

An unmarried man is concerned about the Lord's affairs—how he can please the Lord. But a married man is concerned about the affairs of this world—how he can please his wife—and his interests are divided. An unmarried woman or virgin is concerned about the Lord's affairs: Her aim is to be devoted to the Lord in both body and spirit. But a married woman is concerned about the affairs of this world—how she can please her husband (1 Corinthians 7:32-34).

If you are dating someone seriously, you have three options in the future: keep dating, break up, or move on toward marriage. This chapter deals with moving on toward marriage. Solomon wrote, "He who finds a wife finds what is good and receives favor from the Lord" (Proverbs 18:22). The writer of Hebrews wrote, "Marriage should be honored by all, and the marriage bed kept pure" (Hebrews 13:4).

Remaining single is not more honorable than getting married; nor is the opposite true. In 1 Corinthians 7, Paul makes it clear that the choice is up to us. *You* have to decide whether you want to marry or not.

RATIONAL COURTSHIP

Courtship is the period in the dating relationship where plans to get married are begun. In his book *Love and Sex Are Not Enough* (Herald Press), Charles DeSanto uses the term "rational courtship." This expresses the fact that the love side of your triangle is a cognitive, or thinking, side. Of course, your courtship will involve your motives and emotions, but it also must involve your mind.

In contrast, let's first examine an irrational courtship. We've looked at Samson as an example of someone who was a loser at picking women. Scripture tells of his spending the night with a prostitute (Judges 16:1). Later he fell in love with Delilah, and she caused his downfall (Judges 16:4-21).

Even his wife betrayed his deepest secrets (Judges 14:10-20). It's not surprising, considering how Samson went about picking his wife.

Samson went down to Timnah and saw there a young Philistine woman. When he returned, he said to his father and mother, "I have seen a

Philistine woman in Timnah; now get her for me as my wife."

His father and mother replied, "Isn't there an acceptable woman among your relatives or among all our people? Must you go to the uncircumcised Philistines to get a wife?"

But Samson said to his father, "Get her for me. She's the right one for me" (Judges 14:1-3).

Samson was sure this woman was the one for him even though she was from a different background, his parents disapproved, and he really didn't know her. It was love at first sight! In fact, it appears that it was *only* first sight. A few verses later when Samson went with his mother and father to arrange the wedding, we read, "Then he went down and talked with the woman, and he liked her" (Judges 14:7). At least it was good that he liked her after he talked with her!

Contrast that courtship with the courtship of Isaac and Rebekah (which we looked at in chapter 7). In this courtship, both Isaac's and Rebekah's families approved of the marriage. Rebekah was from the right cultural, religious, and family background. She was a hospitable, sexually pure, kind, modest, hardworking, beautiful woman.

Isaac was from a similar cultural, family, and religious background. He had the financial means to support them as a family. And when he met the woman his father's servant had brought for him, "Isaac brought her into the tent of his mother Sarah, and he married Rebekah. So she became his wife, and he loved her" (Genesis 24:67).

Samson's marriage lasted the seven days of the

wedding feast. His wife cried the whole time (Judges 14:17). Isaac's marriage lasted a lifetime. When a problem arose, "Isaac prayed to the Lord on behalf of his wife, because she was barren. The Lord answered his prayer, and his wife Rebekah became pregnant" (Genesis 25:21).

Isaac and Rebekah's marriage was not without serious conflict. But with a strong basis in their rational courtship, they overcame their marriage problems. They lived together for life, and were buried together in a cave in a field in Canaan (Genesis 49:30-31). What a contrast to Samson's week of marriage!

I'm sure none of you want to go back to the system where parents pick marriage partners. However, as you are courting, you certainly should consider the same things parents of the past did. Although your parents won't pick your future spouse, you should ask their advice and get their approval whenever you begin to get serious about someone.

ENGAGEMENT

In our culture, the next step after courtship is engagement. To engage means to make a pledge or a promise. When you get engaged, you promise to marry the other person. When this happens, the love (commitment) side of your triangle increases markedly. Just as your triangle changed greatly when you had your first date and lengthened slowly as you continued to date, now it changes greatly again.

When you're going together you might talk about "if we get married." When you're engaged, the "if" is gone, and the word becomes "when." You've made a commitment to the other person, and you begin to make definite plans for your marriage.

As you make these plans, you'll find out more about the values and goals of your future spouse. Plans for the wedding itself take time, so begin well ahead. Talk together about when it will be, and who will be invited. Agree on who will pay for what. This is cold, cognitive, and businesslike, but it's all a necessary part of the love side of your triangle.

Talk about the role of money in your marriage. Disagreement about money is one of the leading causes of divorce. Plan accordingly ahead of time. You'll need several thousand dollars—and some very practical wedding gifts—to get started. Find out about the cost of an apartment, insurance on your furniture and car, food, and utilities (gas, electricity, water, phone, and garbage collection). Then compare these costs with your income. Is your income greater than your expenses? If not, wait until it is before you get married.

Talk about sex in your marriage as the wedding day approaches. Read several books on Christian marriage that deal candidly with sex. Discuss how you feel about what you read. With society's great emphasis on sex, disagreements about it are another leading cause of divorce.

Spend time with each other's families. Of course, you did this when you were dating, but be sure to do it even more when you're engaged. You should become accustomed to the way the family does things since you'll be spending time with them after you're married.

Talk about children. Do you want any? If so, how many? Do you want to have them soon after marriage, or later in life? Do you and your future spouse agree on how to raise children and how to discipline them?

Finally, go to someone for premarital counseling. That person should know you both well enough, but still be objective enough to point out possible problems and help you solve them before the marriage.

One thing that may sound logical, but just doesn't work, is living together before marriage while you're engaged. The *reasoning* behind living together is that the two of you can get adjusted to each other before you marry, thus making marriage better. The *fact* is that your marriage will be less satisfactory. A recent study by the National Bureau of Economic Research on nearly 5,000 Swedish women found that couples who live together before marriage have nearly an 80 percent higher divorce rate.

Remember that the engagement period is your last chance to change your mind about marriage. You've *agreed* to marry the other person, but you have no *legal commitment* to do so. About half of all engagements are broken—but better a broken engagement than a broken marriage. When I hear about an engaged couple breaking up, I feel sorry for them. However, I feel good that a divorce was probably prevented.

MARRIAGE

The final step in lengthening the love side of your triangle is marriage. Just as this side suddenly increases when you begin to date a person and when you become engaged, it also increases when you marry. When you marry, you make several commitments.

Marriage is a strong *personal* commitment. In the traditional wedding vows, the husband and wife each promise to take the other "for better, for worse, for richer, for poorer, in sickness and in health, to love and to cherish, till death do us part." When things go from bad to worse, when money runs out, and when you are both sick, you promise to stick with each other—until one of you dies.

The rest of the traditional marriage ceremony is filled with words related to thinking and deciding. The couple is instructed not to marry "unadvisedly," and people in attendance are asked if there is "just cause" that the couple should not marry. At the beginning of the ceremony the couple makes a "covenant," a "pledge of faith," and "solemn vows."

The ceremony has virtually nothing in it about sex or dating. The couple promises to comfort and cherish each other. The ceremony has nothing in it about a couple staying together as long as they feel close to each other. The promises a couple makes are cognitive, not motivational or emotional.

Marriage is also a strong *legal* commitment. In fact, it is the most binding legal contract you can make in our society. You can't even enter this contract without permission (a marriage license) from the state. You can't enter the contract without an officer of the state (a minister or justice of the peace) approving. In addition, two other people must witness your agreement. Can you think of any other contract like that?

Once you enter into this legal partnership, you become responsible for nearly everything the other person does. If he or she buys something on credit, you are legally responsible to pay for it. If you decide you want to break the contract and get a divorce, you can't just break the contract yourselves, even if you both agree. To break it, you must have permission (the approval of a judge) from the state.

Even if you formally break the contract with the approval of the state, you may still have lifelong legal obligations. You may have to pay alimony—women as well as men. You may have to pay child support. Even with our modern "no-fault" divorce laws, you are really making lifetime legal commitments to the other person.

Marriage is also a strong *spiritual* commitment. In the first book of the Old Testament we saw that it was not good for Adam to be alone, so God made Eve. Then we read that a man will leave his father and mother and be united to his wife (Genesis 2:24).

This unity is like grafting a tree. The couple become one in Christ. Two people actually grow together. Just as you cannot tear apart a grafted tree, you cannot break a marriage commitment without seriously hurting both people.

In the first book of the New Testament, the Pharisees asked Jesus about breaking the marriage commitment.

> "Haven't you read," He replied, "that at the beginning the Creator 'made them male and female,' and said, 'For this reason a man will leave his father and mother and be united to his wife, and the two will become one flesh'? So they are no longer two, but one. Therefore what God has joined together, let man not separate" (Matthew 19:4-6).

The Apostle Paul says, "To the married I give this

command (not I, but the Lord): A wife must not separate from her husband. . . . And a husband must not
divorce his wife" (1 Corinthians 7:10-11). The Bible is
clear that God's will is marriage for life. Marriage is a
promise to another person in the presence of your
whole society and God Himself.

THE TRIANGLE COMPLETED

When you marry, your triangle becomes large and balanced. You make a lifetime commitment to the other
person. You have God's blessing on sexual relations
with that person. You can share anything with that
person, secure in knowing that he or she has made a
lifetime commitment to you.

The challenge for you then is to keep the triangle
large and balanced. Even when married, it's still possible for any or all sides of the triangle to become short-
ened, or for the triangle to be completely broken.

On the other hand, your triangle can continue to
grow throughout life. You can show your commitment
to your spouse by sticking with him or her in the
toughest situations. As you each become more and
more convinced of each other's commitment in this
world where many people don't keep commitments,
you'll both grow to become better persons.

In a committed relationship, maximum sharing is
possible. If you know that, no matter what you share
with another person, he or she will stick with you, you
are free to share anything. As the other person keeps
your confidences, you can become more and more
open with him or her.

As you think about your love triangle, remember
that if you keep the sides about equal as it slowly

develops, it can grow into a Christian marriage. The ideal growth rate of your love triangle is represented in the following figure.

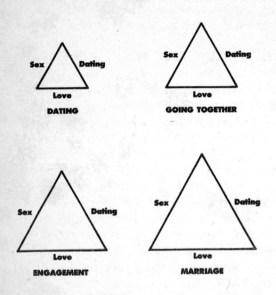

Notice how all three sides grow equally throughout the dating, going together, engagement, and marriage stages of a relationship. Throughout adolescence, as the sides become unequal, it's up to you to make them equal again. Your goal is a Christian marriage relationship—the maximum love triangle with love, sex, and dating at their best.